"DINNER" UNDER PRESSURE

ALSO BY LAURA ARNOLD:

INSTANT ONE-POT MEALS

BEST SIMPLE SUPPERS FOR TWO

BEST SWEETS & TREATS FOR TWO

LAURA ARNOLD

DINNER UNDER PRESSURE

6-INGREDIENT

INSTANT ONE-POT

MEALS

THE COUNTRYMAN PRESS
A division of W. W. Norton & Company
Independent Publishers Since 1923

CONTENTS

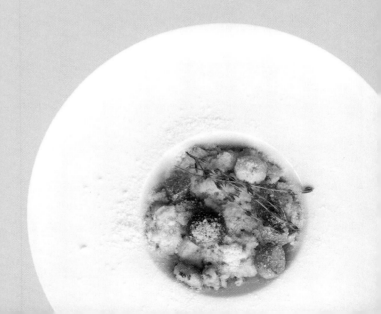

INTRODUCTION

Getting dinner on the table can seem like a daunting task. Not only do you have to shop for the ingredients, but then you have to unload, chop, and finally cook everything, hoping to get a delicious dish after being tired from a long day of work. One-pot meals have changed the dinner game plan, making dinner seamless and easy, especially with only one vessel to clean. The electric pressure cooker has also become a wildly popular device for busy singles, families, and couples alike to be able to cook their favorite recipes in half the time on a busy weeknight, or even for larger groups on the weekend, stress-free and hands-free. The only problem with one-pot recipes and pressure-cooking recipes is that, oftentimes, it feels like there are so many ingredients and steps just to get an "easy" meal finished quickly on a weeknight.

Dinner Under Pressure was created with the mind-set of the busy individual who wants a delicious, crowd-pleasing dish that satisfies any age group and any number of people in only a matter of minutes. Using just six ingredients (wow!), you can create some of your favorite recipes, such as Classic Meat Loaf, Butternut Squash Risotto, Chicken Carbonara, and Chicken Cordon Bleu, so easily. The key to *Dinner Under Pressure* is the homemade Spice Mixes & Sauces (pages 151–165) that boost any dish to a new flavor level. Use these recipes or store-bought spice blends and sauces for recipe success throughout this book. Also, *Dinner Under Pressure* likes to utilize fresh or frozen meat, starch, and veggie options throughout the book so you can buy in advance and come home already prepared to cook a delicious meal. When you feel like you are in a dinner pinch, the time-saving recipes and tips throughout *Dinner Under Pressure* will help you succeed in getting a meal that tastes as delicious as if it took you all day! Forget frozen pizza or Chinese delivery—say yes to making homemade dinners a reality!

TROUBLESHOOTING RECIPES WITH THE PRESSURE COOKER

When using the electric pressure cooker, it is important to understand some key tricks to help you create a successful recipe. Be sure to refer to your manual about the correct way to use the pressure cooker and always face the steam valve away from you! Within this book are a number of recipes, such as casseroles and pastas, that use thicker sauces. With thicker sauces and cream sauces, there is a chance they could possibly burn in the bottom of the pressure cooker. To avoid burning anything in the pressure cooker, it is essential to use the steamer rack as well as a 7-cup heatproof glass baking dish (such as Pyrex), 6- or 7-inch cake pan, or 3-quart smaller pressure cooker insert. Fill the pressure cooker with 1 cup of water and place the steamer rack inside. Place the casserole dish on top of the steamer rack and the steam will allow the casserole to cook perfectly.

Another question often asked with the pressure cooker is how to make sure every recipe will come to pressure correctly. The amount of liquid in a recipe is essential for pressure to be attained. Each recipe needs to have at least ½ to ¾ cup of liquid for the pressure cooker to work correctly. In addition, be sure that the steam valve is locked and closed when setting the pressure cooker settings, as an open valve will allow air to come through into the machine and the correct pressure will never be reached.

After a recipe has finished cooking and the pot has been opened, the sauce or ingredients may seem thin or watery. This problem can be solved by returning the pressure cooker to the SAUTÉ setting and bringing the sauce to a simmer. Allow the sauce to simmer until it has thickened and reduced to the desired consistency before serving.

RECIPE TIMING

When setting the cook time for the electric pressure cooker, the machine doesn't begin the pressure cooking immediately. The machine first needs to build enough steam pressure inside the cooking chamber. The time that the machine takes to come to pressure can take anywhere from 10 to 15 minutes, depending on the amount of ingredients and liquid inside the pressure cooker. This will add additional hands-off wait time while you are making any pressure cooker recipe.

Additionally, when the machine is finished cooking, it will beep and the KEEP WARM function will turn on. (Hit the CANCEL button to turn the machine off; oftentimes, the KEEP WARM setting can cause your food to burn.) This is the time in which you can choose either natural release, partial natural release, or quick release. Natural release is when you allow the pressure valve to release by itself without touching

the machine; this could take another 15 minutes or so. Partial release, which is often used in this book, is when you allow the machine to naturally release for a certain number of minutes and then you quick release to hasten the process and release the steam valve. Quick release is when you manually release the pressure valve to release all of the steam immediately and remove the lid. The type of release for each recipe is indicated in the method.

When looking at the cooking times in these recipes, the pressure time and active time are the only times indicated. This means that there is an additional 15 to 30 minutes of additional hands-free time in which the machine needs to come to pressure and/or release pressure in a certain way. It is important to understand and note this when recipe planning.

THE KEY IS SPICE MIXES AND SAUCES!

When making recipes that are just six ingredients, oftentimes people worry that the recipes will turn out bland and have no flavor. The key to flavor-boosting recipes is using spices and sauces to add that made-from-scratch touch. The final chapter contains recipes for several homemade spice mixes and sauces that take only a couple of minutes to make. Label and store these spice mixes and sauces to use in delicious recipes throughout this book (I like to make the sauces in big batches and store them in the freezer for easy weeknight prep!). You can also use these sauces and spice mixes in recipes that you don't pressure cook, which serves a double purpose!

It is often hard to find time to make sauces and spice mixes during the week, so another time-saving alternative is to find the store-bought versions of these items to use in the recipes. The store-bought versions of the items are often mentioned as options in the ingredient lists.

CHICKEN & SEAFOOD

PULLED CHICKEN TACOS

Taco night is always one of my favorites and the leftovers make the perfect lunch the next day. Try making this easy and delicious taco recipe that next time you are planning for taco night.

Prep time: 5 minutes | Cook time: 8 minutes (MANUAL) + 2 minutes (SAUTÉ) | Serves 4

PRIMARY INGREDIENTS
4 boneless, skinless chicken breasts
One 16-ounce jar mild salsa
One 15-ounce can black beans, drained and rinsed
1 cup frozen corn

ON-HAND INGREDIENTS
2 teaspoons kosher salt
½ teaspoon freshly ground black pepper
1 cup water
1 tablespoon Mexican Spice Mix (page 152), or store-bought equivalent

TO SERVE
Eight to ten 6-inch corn tortillas
1 bunch cilantro, chopped, for garnish

Season the chicken breasts with the salt and pepper on both sides. Place 1 cup water, spice mix, and chicken breasts in the pressure cooker and top with the salsa. Secure the lid and place on MANUAL with high pressure for 8 minutes. Allow to naturally release for 5 minutes, then quick release and remove the lid. Shred the chicken, using two forks. Select the SAUTÉ setting and stir in the black beans and corn. Allow to simmer until warmed through, about 2 minutes. Season with additional salt and pepper, if necessary. Serve in corn tortillas, garnished with chopped cilantro.

ORANGE CHICKEN AND VEGETABLES

I'll be the first to admit, I am weak when it comes to Chinese takeout—it's delicious, especially after a long day of work. But this recipe can change your takeout game. With just a couple of ingredients, you can have takeout night in your own kitchen.

Prep time: 5 minutes | Cook time: 9 minutes (SAUTÉ) + 5 minutes (MANUAL) | Serves 4

PRIMARY INGREDIENTS

6 boneless, skinless chicken thighs, cut into 1-inch pieces
One 14-ounce bag frozen stir-fry vegetables
¼ cup soy sauce
⅔ cup BBQ Sauce (page 161), or store-bought BBQ sauce
¾ cup store-bought orange marmalade

ON-HAND INGREDIENTS

2 tablespoons olive oil
2 teaspoons freshly ground black pepper
½ cup water

TO SERVE

2 cups frozen cooked white rice, steamed
Sliced scallions, for garnish (optional)

Select the SAUTÉ setting and heat the olive oil in the pressure cooker. Season the chicken on all sides with the pepper. Add the chicken to the pot and sear on all sides until browned, about 6 minutes. Add the stir-fry vegetables and cook for another 3 minutes. Add ½ cup water, soy sauce, BBQ sauce, and marmalade, but do not stir to combine. Secure the lid and set on MANUAL with high pressure for 5 minutes. Use quick release and remove the lid. Serve over steamed white rice and garnish with scallions, if desired.

CHICKEN AND WILD RICE CASSEROLE

There is nothing more comforting in the wintertime than a bowl of chicken and wild rice soup. This recipe takes that classic soup and turns it into a casserole that anyone will love.

Prep time: 5 minutes | Cook time: 5 minutes (MANUAL) + 2 minutes (SAUTÉ) | Serves 4

PRIMARY INGREDIENTS

1 cup chicken stock

Two 8.5-ounce bags parcooked wild rice and brown rice blend

½ rotisserie chicken, skin and bones removed and discarded, shredded

2 carrots, sliced in rounds, or ½ cup frozen sliced carrots

1½ cups Cream Sauce (page 165), or store-bought cream sauce

ON-HAND INGREDIENTS

1 tablespoon Lemon Herb Spice Mix (page 157), or store-bought equivalent

Place all the ingredients, except the cream sauce, in the pressure cooker; do not stir. Secure the lid and cook on MANUAL with high pressure for 5 minutes. Use quick release and remove the lid. Select the SAUTÉ setting and stir in the cream sauce. Allow to warm through, about 2 minutes, and serve.

CHICKEN CORDON BLEU

A true classic dish that everyone loves—I decided to try this in my pressure cooker after we made a version on *The Chew*, and wow!—it is way too easy.

Prep time: 15 minutes | Cook time: 8 minutes (MANUAL) | Serves 4

PRIMARY INGREDIENTS

¾ cup chicken stock

8 chicken cutlets

6 ounces thinly sliced deli ham

2 cups shredded Gruyère

ON-HAND INGREDIENTS

Cooking spray

2 teaspoons kosher salt

½ teaspoon freshly ground black pepper

TO SERVE

1 recipe Herbed Bread Crumbs (page 158), or store-bought herbed bread crumbs

Place the steamer rack in the pressure cooker and add the chicken stock. Place a piece of foil on top of the steamer rack to cover and spray with cooking spray.

Season the chicken cutlets on both sides with the salt and pepper. Place one slice of ham on top of the cutlet, sprinkle with the cheese, and roll up like a jelly roll until closed. Seal with a toothpick. Repeat with remaining ham, cheese, and chicken for a total of eight chicken rolls.

Place the chicken rolls on top of the foil on the steamer rack. Secure the lid and place on MANUAL with high pressure for 8 minutes. Allow to naturally release for 5 minutes, then quick release and remove the lid. Allow the chicken rolls to cool for 10 minutes.

Remove the chicken rolls from the pressure cooker and discard the toothpicks. Sprinkle the top of the chicken rolls with the herbed bread crumbs and serve.

CHICKEN CACCIATORE

Living in New York, there is a lot of great Italian food that I crave on a daily basis. This classic Italian recipe is just as easy to make on a weeknight in your pressure cooker. Try using frozen chicken thighs if you are in a pinch!

Prep time: 5 minutes | Cook time: 15 minutes (SAUTÉ) + 15 minutes (MANUAL) | Serves 4

PRIMARY INGREDIENTS

4 or 5 bone-in skin-on chicken thighs
One 14-ounce bag frozen or prechopped
   mixed onion and bell peppers
2 teaspoons dried rosemary
4 garlic cloves, minced, or 2 teaspoons
   jarred minced garlic
2 cups Tomato Sauce (page 162), or
   store-bought tomato sauce
¼ cup pitted oil-cured Italian black olives
   or Kalamata olives

ON-HAND INGREDIENTS

2 tablespoons olive oil
2 teaspoons kosher salt
1 teaspoon freshly ground black pepper

Select the SAUTÉ setting and heat the olive oil in the pressure cooker. Season the chicken thighs with the salt and pepper. Add the chicken to the pot and sear skin-side down until golden brown, about 7 minutes. Flip and sear an additional 3 minutes. Transfer the thighs to a plate. Add the onion and bell pepper mixture to the pressure cooker and cook for 4 minutes. Add the rosemary and garlic and cook for an additional minute. Add the tomato sauce, secure the lid, and place on MANUAL with high pressure for 15 minutes. Allow to naturally release for 5 minutes, then quick release and remove the lid. Stir in the olives and serve.

Tip: If you want to cook frozen chicken thighs, be sure to cook on MANUAL with high pressure for 25 minutes, or until cooked through and a meat thermometer registers 165°F.

GREEN CHICKEN ENCHILADAS

I love entertaining, and when having people over, you want to choose a dish that is definitely going to be a crowd-pleaser. Enchiladas are one of my favorite weeknight entertaining dishes. These enchiladas are so easy, you will never be stressed when it comes to having a friend or two over for dinner.

Prep time: 10 minutes | Cook time: 5 minutes (MANUAL) | Serves 4

PRIMARY INGREDIENTS

Two 15-ounce cans green enchilada sauce
½ rotisserie chicken, skin removed and discarded, shredded
1 cup refried beans
Ten 6-inch corn tortillas
1 cup shredded pepper Jack cheese

ON-HAND INGREDIENTS

1 cup water
2 tablespoons Mexican Spice Mix (page 152), or store-bought equivalent

Add 1 cup water to the pressure cooker and place steamer rack inside. Pour one can of the enchilada sauce into a 7-cup heatproof glass baking dish. Mix together the chicken and Mexican seasoning in a large bowl. Spread 1 to 2 tablespoons of refried beans in the center of a tortilla and top with about ¼ cup of the shredded chicken mixture. Roll up each tortilla to close and place, seam side down, in the baking dish. Repeat with the remaining chicken mixture and beans, stacking the rolled tortillas on top of each other if necessary. Pour the remaining can of enchilada sauce over the rolled tortillas and top with the shredded cheese. Place the baking dish in the pressure cooker. Secure the lid and place on MANUAL with high pressure for 5 minutes. Quick release and remove the lid. Serve immediately.

CHICKEN WITH CRANBERRY SAUCE

Cranberry Sauce is my favorite Thanksgiving "side" my mom makes every year. While the canned sauce is tasty, making the sauce from scratch is crazy delicious. This recipe lets you have that flavor all year long.

Prep time: 2 minutes | Cook time: 8 minutes (SAUTÉ) + 8 minutes (MANUAL) | Serves 4

PRIMARY INGREDIENTS
6 bone-in skin-on chicken thighs
1 teaspoon dried thyme
½ cup chicken stock
One 10-ounce bag frozen cranberries
3 tablespoons sugar (or more if you don't like it too tart!)

ON-HAND INGREDIENTS
2 tablespoons olive oil
2 teaspoons kosher salt
½ teaspoon freshly ground black pepper

Select the SAUTÉ setting and heat the olive oil in the pressure cooker. Season the chicken thighs on both sides with salt and pepper. Place, skin-side down, and sear until both sides are golden brown, about 4 minutes per side. Add the thyme during the last minute of cooking. Deglaze the pan with the chicken stock and add the cranberries and sugar. Secure the lid and place on MANUAL with high pressure for 8 minutes. Quick release and remove the lid. Return to SAUTÉ if the sauce needs to thicken and allow to simmer until desired consistency.

CAJUN CHICKEN LETTUCE CUPS

To me, this recipe is an easy and delicious summertime dinner that is also so versatile. To switch this dish up, try using pork or beef instead with grilled or roasted veggies!

Prep time: 5 minutes | Cook time: 9 minutes (SAUTÉ) + 4 minutes (MANUAL) | Serves 4

PRIMARY INGREDIENTS

1½ pounds raw chicken tenders, cut in half if too long
Half of one 14-ounce bag frozen or prechopped mixed onion and bell peppers
¼ cup chicken stock

ON-HAND INGREDIENTS

2 tablespoons olive oil
1 tablespoon Cajun Spice Mix (page 154), or store-bought equivalent
1 teaspoon kosher salt
½ teaspoon freshly ground black pepper

TO SERVE

1 head Bibb lettuce, leaves separated
1 cup shredded carrot, for garnish
½ bunch scallions, thinly sliced, for garnish

Select the SAUTÉ setting and heat the olive oil in the pressure cooker. Season the chicken tenders with the Cajun spice mix, salt, and pepper in a large bowl. Add the chicken to the pot and cook until seared on all sides, about 5 minutes. Transfer the chicken to a plate. Add the onion and pepper mixture and cook until slightly softened, about 4 minutes. Deglaze the pan with the chicken stock, secure the lid, and place on MANUAL with high pressure for 4 minutes. Use quick release and remove the lid. Serve the chicken in Bibb lettuce leaves garnished with shredded carrots and scallions.

*Tip: Try using frozen chicken tenders. Cook on **MANUAL** with high pressure for 10 minutes, or until cooked through and a meat thermometer registers 165°F.*

CHICKEN RAMEN

As one of my favorite wintertime soups to eat out in New York City, this ramen is an easy version for your pressure cooker. Customize your ramen with your preferred proteins and veggies.

Prep time: 8 minutes | Cook time: 4 minutes (SAUTÉ) + 8 minutes (MANUAL) + 5 minutes (SAUTÉ) | Serves 4

PRIMARY INGREDIENTS

1 bunch scallions, thinly sliced, divided

2 tablespoons peeled and minced fresh ginger

6 cups beef stock

⅓ cup reduced-sodium soy sauce

6 boneless, skinless chicken thighs, cut into thin strips

8 ounces ramen, soba, or udon

ON-HAND INGREDIENTS

2 tablespoons olive oil

TO SERVE

4 store-bought or homemade hard-boiled eggs, halved (optional)

Select the SAUTÉ setting and heat the olive oil in the pressure cooker. Add half of the scallions and all of the ginger and cook until softened, about 4 minutes. Add the beef stock, soy sauce, and chicken. Secure the lid and cook on MANUAL with high pressure for 8 minutes. Use quick release and remove the lid. Select the SAUTÉ setting and bring the stock to a simmer. Add the noodles and allow to simmer until cooked through, about 5 minutes. Transfer to four bowls and top each with an egg and more scallions.

LEMON, PEPPER, AND HERB WHOLE CHICKEN

This is a weeknight recipe I love making whenever I am meal prepping for the week ahead. I use the leftover chicken in soups, salads, and casseroles.

Prep time: 15 minutes | Cook time: 13 minutes (SAUTÉ) + 25 minutes (MANUAL) | Serves 4

PRIMARY INGREDIENTS
One 3- to 4-pound whole chicken
1 lemon, thinly sliced
1½ pounds baby Yukon gold potatoes, halved if too large
½ cup chicken stock

ON-HAND INGREDIENTS
2 tablespoons olive oil
1 tablespoon Lemon Herb Spice Mix (page 157), or store-bought equivalent
2 teaspoons kosher salt
½ teaspoon freshly ground black pepper

Select the SAUTÉ setting and heat the olive oil in the pressure cooker. Stuff the cavity of the chicken with the lemon slices. Tie the legs of the chicken together with butcher's twine. Season the outside of the chicken with the lemon herb spice mix, salt, and pepper. Place in the pressure cooker and sear on all sides until golden brown, 8 to 10 minutes. Transfer to a plate. Add the potatoes to the pressure cooker and cook until golden brown, about 5 minutes. Add the chicken stock and the chicken back to the pressure cooker, secure the lid, and set on MANUAL with high pressure for 25 minutes. Allow to naturally release for 5 minutes, then quick release and remove the lid. Allow the chicken to rest for 10 to 15 minutes, then cut into parts and serve with the potatoes.

CHICKEN AND RICE

Chicken and rice was one of my favorite dishes as a child. This is an international spin on the classic weeknight dinner.

Prep time: 5 minutes | Cook time: 13 minutes (SAUTÉ) + 25 minutes (MANUAL) | Serves 4

PRIMARY INGREDIENTS

4 bone-in, skin-on chicken thighs

4 chicken drumsticks

One 14-ounce bag frozen or prechopped mixed onion and bell peppers

1½ cups chicken stock

1 cup uncooked long-grain white rice, rinsed

One 15-ounce can diced tomatoes

ON-HAND INGREDIENTS

2 tablespoons olive oil

2 teaspoons kosher salt

½ teaspoon freshly ground black pepper

1 tablespoon plus 2 teaspoons Mexican Spice Mix (page 152), or store-bought equivalent

Select the SAUTÉ setting and heat the olive oil in the pressure cooker. Season the chicken on all sides with the salt and pepper. Add the chicken to the pot and sear until golden brown on all sides, about 8 minutes—you may need to sear the chicken in batches. Transfer to a plate. Add the onion and pepper mixture and cook until softened, about 4 minutes. Add the Mexican spice mix and cook for another minute. Add the chicken stock, rice, seared chicken, and tomatoes, in that order, to the pressure cooker. Secure the lid and set on MANUAL with high pressure for 25 minutes. Allow to naturally release for 5 minutes, then quick release and remove the lid. Stir thoroughly and return to the SAUTÉ setting if necessary to thicken the sauce slightly. Serve.

CHICKEN DIVAN

Broccoli, rice, and chicken casserole in a creamy, cheesy sauce—this classic is tried and true for both kids and adults. Try switching up the vegetable for a new take on this dish!

Prep time: 5 minutes | Cook time: 6 minutes (SAUTÉ) + 8 minutes (MANUAL) | Serves 4

PRIMARY INGREDIENTS

2 boneless, skinless chicken breasts, cut into 1-inch pieces (about 1 pound)

12 ounces fresh broccoli florets, or one 12-ounce bag frozen broccoli florets

One 10-ounce bag frozen, cooked white rice

2 cups Cream Sauce (page 165), or store-bought cream sauce

1½ cups shredded cheddar

ON-HAND INGREDIENTS

2 tablespoons olive oil

2 teaspoons kosher salt

½ teaspoon freshly ground black pepper

1 cup water

Cooking spray

1 cup Herbed Bread Crumbs (page 158), or store-bought herbed bread crumbs

Select the SAUTÉ setting and heat the olive oil in the pressure cooker. Season the chicken with the salt and pepper. Add the chicken to the pot and cook on all sides until browned, 6 to 8 minutes. Transfer to a plate. Wipe out the inside of the pressure cooker. Place the steamer rack inside the pressure cooker and add 1 cup water. Spray the 3-quart insert or a 7-cup heatproof glass baking dish with cooking spray. Place the broccoli, white rice, cream sauce, and seared chicken in the prepared insert or baking dish and stir to combine. Secure the lid and cook on MANUAL with high pressure for 8 minutes. Quick release and remove the lid. Stir the cheddar into the casserole until melted. Sprinkle the top with the herbed bread crumbs and serve.

Tip: Buy chicken breasts, cut into cubes, and freeze in an even layer so the pieces don't clump together. Then, cook from frozen in the casserole on *MANUAL* with high pressure for 14 minutes, or until cooked through and a meat thermometer registers 165°F.

KING RANCH CHICKEN CASSEROLE

I hadn't tried this casserole until a couple of years ago and I suddenly realized why it's a true crowd-pleaser. It's like combining tacos and Tex-Mex all into one delicious dish. Try making this recipe with shredded pork or beef for a new spin on the flavors.

Prep time: 5 minutes | Cook time: 10 minutes (SAUTÉ) + 6 minutes (MANUAL) | Serves 4

PRIMARY INGREDIENTS
2 boneless, skinless chicken breasts, cubed
One 10-ounce bag frozen mixed onion and bell peppers
Two 15-ounce cans cream of chicken soup or 2 cups Cream Sauce (page 165)
One 10-ounce can diced tomatoes with green chiles
Ten 6-inch corn tortillas, torn
¾ cup shredded cheddar

ON-HAND INGREDIENTS
2 tablespoons olive oil
2 tablespoons Mexican Spice Mix (page 152), or store-bought equivalent
2 teaspoons kosher salt
½ teaspoon freshly ground black pepper
½ cup water

Select the SAUTÉ setting and heat the olive oil in the pressure cooker. Place the chicken in a bowl and toss with the spice mix until coated. Add the chicken to the pot and cook until browned on all sides, about 6 minutes. Add the onion and pepper mixture and cook until translucent, about 4 minutes. Season with the salt and pepper. Add the cream of chicken soup and tomatoes and mix to combine. Add the torn corn tortillas and ½ cup water and stir to combine. Secure the lid and cook on MANUAL with high pressure for 6 minutes. Use quick release and remove the lid. Shred the chicken using 2 forks, if desired. Sprinkle with cheese and allow to melt before serving.

FARRO WITH CHICKEN SAUSAGE, BUTTERNUT SQUASH, AND CRANBERRIES

Grain bowls are one of my go-to weeknight meals. They are so healthy and versatile. Choose veggies that are in season and pair with dried or fresh fruit for a delicious sweet and savory flavor combination.

Prep time: 5 minutes | Cook time: 7 minutes (SAUTÉ) + 10 minutes (MANUAL) | Serves 4

PRIMARY INGREDIENTS
1 pound chicken sausage, thinly sliced
2 cups frozen or fresh precut butternut squash
½ cup dried cranberries
1½ cups farro, rinsed
1¼ cups chicken stock

ON-HAND INGREDIENTS
2 tablespoons olive oil
1 tablespoon Lemon Herb Spice Mix (page 157), or store-bought equivalent

Select the SAUTÉ setting and heat the olive oil in the pressure cooker. Add the chicken sausage and cook until browned, about 7 minutes. Add the butternut squash, spice mix, cranberries, farro, and chicken stock. Secure the lid and set on MANUAL with high pressure for 10 minutes. Allow to naturally release for 5 minutes, then quick release and remove the lid. Fluff the farro with a fork and serve.

POPPY SEED CHICKEN CASSEROLE

I first had this casserole in the South while working with *Southern Living*. With warm chicken in a creamy sauce topped with crunchy butter crackers, this dish sums up everything that is perfect in a comfort food recipe.

Prep time: 5 minutes | Cook time: 9 minutes (MANUAL) | Serves 4

PRIMARY INGREDIENTS

1 rotisserie chicken, skin and bones removed and discarded, shredded
One 15-ounce can cream of chicken soup
1½ cups sour cream
2 teaspoons poppy seeds

ON-HAND INGREDIENTS

Cooking spray

TO SERVE

2 cups crushed butter crackers

Grease a 7-cup heatproof glass baking dish with cooking spray. Combine the chicken shreds, cream of chicken soup, sour cream, and poppy seeds in the baking dish and place in the pressure cooker. Secure the lid and cook on MANUAL with high pressure for 9 minutes. Allow to naturally release for 5 minutes, then quick release and remove the lid. Sprinkle with crushed butter crackers to finish and serve.

PESTO CHICKEN MEATBALLS AND PENNE

I love this recipe because it is packed full of flavor and so easy to make—you won't believe it! Everyone will think you spent twice the amount of time making this meatball dish.

Prep time: 15 minutes | Cook time: 5 minutes (MANUAL) | Serves 4

PRIMARY INGREDIENTS

1 pound ground chicken

⅓ cup store-bought pesto

1 pound penne

3 cups Tomato Sauce (page 162), or store-bought sauce

ON-HAND INGREDIENTS

½ cup Herbed Bread Crumbs (page 158), or store-bought herbed bread crumbs

2 teaspoons kosher salt

½ teaspoon freshly ground black pepper

1 cup water

TO SERVE

½ cup grated Parmesan

Mix the ground chicken, pesto, bread crumbs, salt, and pepper together in a large bowl. Form the chicken mixture into 1-inch balls and place on a plate. Place the penne, 1 cup water, and tomato sauce in the pressure cooker. Drop the meatballs into the sauce. Secure the lid and place on MANUAL with high pressure for 5 minutes. Allow to naturally release for 5 minutes, then quick release and remove the lid. Serve with grated Parmesan.

BUFFALO CHICKEN PENNE

Who doesn't love anything that is buffalo chicken?! When I tested this recipe, it quickly became one of my favorites in the book. It is creamy, cheesy, and delicious, with a kick of spice that will have everyone asking for seconds.

Prep time: 5 minutes | Cook time: 4 minutes (MANUAL) + 3 minutes (SAUTÉ) | Serves 4

PRIMARY INGREDIENTS

1 rotisserie chicken, skin removed and discarded, shredded
⅓ cup hot sauce
1 pound penne
1½ cups Cream Sauce (page 165), or store-bought cream sauce
1 cup shredded cheddar

ON-HAND INGREDIENTS

1 tablespoon Cajun Spice Mix (page 154), or store-bought equivalent
2 teaspoons kosher salt
½ teaspoon freshly ground black pepper
2 cups water

Add the chicken, hot sauce, pasta, spice mix, salt, pepper, and water to the bowl of the pressure cooker. Mix to combine. Secure the lid and set on MANUAL with high pressure for 4 minutes. Quick release and remove the lid. Select the SAUTÉ setting, add the cream sauce, and stir until warmed through, about 3 minutes. Stir in the cheddar until melted and serve.

PINEAPPLE BBQ CHICKEN

Using pineapple and other summer fruits in savory dishes is one of my favorite seasonal recipe tricks. With this recipe, you can use either fresh or frozen pineapple to make it for dinner all year round.

Prep time: 5 minutes | Cook time: 6 minutes (SAUTÉ) + 3 minutes (MANUAL) + 4 minutes (SAUTÉ) | Serves 4

PRIMARY INGREDIENTS

3 boneless, skinless chicken breasts, cut into ½-inch cubes
One 10-ounce bag frozen pineapple chunks
⅓ cup BBQ Sauce (page 161), or store-bought BBQ sauce
⅓ cup chicken stock
One 10-ounce bag frozen cooked white rice

ON-HAND INGREDIENTS

2 tablespoons olive oil
2 teaspoons kosher salt
½ teaspoon freshly ground black pepper

TO SERVE

½ bunch scallions, thinly sliced, for garnish

Select the SAUTÉ setting and heat the olive oil in the pressure cooker. Season the chicken with the salt and pepper. Add the chicken to the pot and sear on all sides until golden, about 6 minutes. Add the pineapple, BBQ sauce, and chicken stock. Secure the lid and place on MANUAL with high pressure for 3 minutes. Allow to naturally release for 5 minutes, then quick release and remove the lid. Select the SAUTÉ setting again, add the rice, and allow to simmer until the rice is warmed and the sauce is slightly thickened, about 4 minutes. Garnish with scallions.

CHICKEN CARBONARA

Are you ready to impress your guests or your family? This dish is the perfect combo of cheesy and creamy—my friends finished the whole pot!

Prep time: 5 minutes | Cook time: 12 minutes (SAUTÉ) + 4 minutes (MANUAL) | Serves 4

PRIMARY INGREDIENTS

5 bacon strips, chopped

2 boneless, skinless chicken breasts, cut into ½-inch cubes

1 pound spaghetti or linguine, broken lengthwise in half

2 large eggs

⅓ cup heavy cream

¾ cup grated Parmesan

ON-HAND INGREDIENTS

3 teaspoons kosher salt

2 teaspoons freshly ground black pepper

3½ cups water

Select the SAUTÉ setting and place the bacon in the pressure cooker. Allow to cook until crispy, 6 to 7 minutes. Transfer the bacon to a paper towel–lined plate and pour all but 1 tablespoon of the bacon drippings out of the pressure cooker. Season the chicken with 2 teaspoons of the salt and 1 teaspoon of the pepper. Add the chicken to the pressure cooker and sear until golden brown on all sides, another 6 minutes. Add the remaining teaspoon of salt and the remaining teaspoon of pepper to the pot along with the spaghetti and 3½ cups water. Secure the lid and cook on MANUAL with high pressure for 4 minutes. Quick release and remove the lid. Meanwhile, whisk together the eggs and cream. Add the egg mixture to the cooked pasta and stir constantly until the sauce thickens. Add the cheese and bacon and stir until the cheese melts.

GREEK CHICKEN WITH POTATOES

When meal prepping, I look for recipes that are versatile and that I can change with just a few simple ingredients. This is just that recipe. Try using a different spice mix; protein, such as turkey or pork; and vegetable to create a new recipe every night of the week.

Prep time: 5 minutes | Cook time: 15 minutes (SAUTÉ) + 8 minutes (MANUAL) | Serves 4

PRIMARY INGREDIENTS

3 small Yukon gold potatoes, cut into
 ½-inch wedges
1 chicken, sectioned into 8 pieces
½ cup chicken stock
4 garlic cloves, smashed

ON-HAND INGREDIENTS

2 tablespoons olive oil
2 teaspoons kosher salt
½ teaspoon freshly ground black pepper
1½ tablespoons Greek Spice Mix
 (page 153), or store-bought equivalent

TO SERVE

1 tablespoon Dijon mustard

Select the SAUTÉ setting and heat the olive oil in the pressure cooker. Season the potatoes with the salt and pepper. Add to the pot and allow to cook until golden brown on both sides, about 6 minutes. Transfer to a plate. Season the chicken with the Greek spice mix. Add the chicken, skin-side down, to the pressure cooker and allow to cook until golden brown, 6 to 7 minutes. Flip and cook for another 3 minutes. Add the chicken stock and garlic. Place the steamer rack on top of the chicken and place the potatoes on top of the rack. Secure the lid and cook on MANUAL with high pressure for 8 minutes. Allow to naturally release for 5 minutes, then quick release and remove the lid. Transfer the chicken and potatoes to a platter. Transfer ½ cup of the mixture at the bottom of the pot to a cup or small bowl and whisk together with the mustard. Serve the mustard sauce over the chicken.

CHICKEN PAD THAI

Asian food can be daunting to make at home—intimidating ingredients often cooked in a complex way. This recipe gives you six simple store-bought ingredients that provide an easy solution to making an involved recipe at home.

Prep time: 10 minutes | Cook time: 5 minutes (SAUTÉ) + 4 minutes (MANUAL) | Serves 4

PRIMARY INGREDIENTS

1 bunch scallions, thinly sliced

Half of one 14-ounce bag frozen or prechopped mixed onion and bell peppers

2 cups rotisserie chicken, skin removed and discarded, shredded

½ cup store-bought pad thai sauce

One 16-ounce package pad thai noodles

ON-HAND INGREDIENTS

2 tablespoons olive oil

1 teaspoon freshly ground black pepper

2½ cups water

TO SERVE

½ cup roasted, salted peanuts, finely chopped, for garnish

Select the SAUTÉ setting and heat the olive oil in the pressure cooker. Add the scallions and cook until almost tender, about 2 minutes. Add the frozen vegetables and cook for another 3 minutes. Add the remaining primary ingredients and then the on-hand ingredients, but do not mix to combine. Secure the lid and place on MANUAL with high pressure for 4 minutes. Quick release and remove the lid. Garnish with the peanuts to serve.

GNOCCHI BAKE

Gnocchi is something I first learned to make when I worked at a restaurant in Charlotte during college. That being said, restaurant-style food is intimidating to try to make at home. This dish gives you all that flavor in an easy home-style recipe! Try adding your favorite sautéed leafy green vegetables to this dish.

Prep time: 8 minutes | Cook time: 8 minutes (MANUAL) | Serves 4

PRIMARY INGREDIENTS

- 1⅓ cups Cream Sauce (page 165), or store-bought Alfredo sauce
- ½ cup grated Parmesan, plus more to serve
- 2 rotisserie chicken breasts, skin removed and discarded, shredded
- One 16-ounce package refrigerated potato gnocchi

ON-HAND INGREDIENTS

- 1 cup water
- 2 teaspoons kosher salt
- ½ teaspoon freshly ground black pepper

Place the steamer rack inside of the pressure cooker and add 1 cup water. Combine the cream sauce and Parmesan in a 7-cup heatproof glass baking dish. Add the chicken, gnocchi, salt, and pepper, stirring to combine. Place the baking dish in the pressure cooker and cover with a piece of foil, secure the lid, and place on MANUAL with high pressure for 8 minutes. Quick release and remove the lid. Serve with additional Parmesan, if desired.

SHRIMP AND ANDOUILLE JAMBALAYA

I remember trying jambalaya for the first time when I was nine years old and never looking back—I was obsessed with the crazy amount of flavor. This jambalaya is simple but full of flavor, between the spicy sausage and tender shrimp.

Prep time: 5 minutes | Cook time: 11 minutes (SAUTÉ) + 8 minutes (MANUAL) + 3 minutes (SAUTÉ) | Serves 4

PRIMARY INGREDIENTS
½ pound andouille sausage, thinly sliced
1 cup frozen or fresh green and red chopped bell peppers
1 cup frozen or fresh diced onion
1¼ cups uncooked long-grain white rice, rinsed
One 14-ounce can crushed tomatoes
¾ pound medium shrimp, peeled, deveined with tails on, or frozen, peeled, cooked shrimp

ON-HAND INGREDIENTS
2 tablespoons olive oil
2 teaspoons kosher salt
1 teaspoon freshly ground black pepper
1 tablespoon Cajun Spice Mix (page 154), or store-bought equivalent
2½ cups water

Select the SAUTÉ setting and heat the olive oil in the pressure cooker. Add the andouille sausage and cook until browned, about 7 minutes. Add the bell peppers and onion and cook for another 4 minutes. Season with the salt, pepper, and Cajun spice mix. Add the rice and stir to coat in the fat. Add 1½ cups of the water and the tomatoes, secure the lid, and place on MANUAL with high pressure for 8 minutes. Use quick release and remove the lid. Return to the SAUTÉ setting, add the remaining cup of water and the shrimp, and cook until the shrimp have turned pink and are cooked through, about 3 minutes. Serve.

TUNA NOODLE CASSEROLE

I have to admit, tuna noodle casserole was a classic dish my grandmother used to make that I never really enjoyed. But I have come to love this version of the recipe in my later years—the herbed bread crumbs give it the perfect crunchy and flavorful topping.

Prep time: 5 minutes | Cook time: 4 minutes (MANUAL) + 3 minutes (SAUTÉ) | Serves 4

PRIMARY INGREDIENTS
One 12-ounce package egg noodles
Two 5-ounce cans tuna packed in water, drained and flaked
1½ cups Cream Sauce (page 165), or one 14-ounce can cream of mushroom soup
1 cup frozen peas
½ cup shredded cheddar

ON-HAND INGREDIENTS
2 cups water
2 teaspoons kosher salt, or no salt if using cream of mushroom soup
1 teaspoon freshly ground black pepper

TO SERVE
½ cup Herbed Bread Crumbs (page 158), or store-bought herbed bread crumbs

Place the egg noodles and 2 cups water in the pressure cooker and season with the salt, if using, and pepper. Add the tuna on top and do not mix. Secure the lid and place on MANUAL with high pressure for 4 minutes. Quick release and remove the lid. Place on the SAUTÉ setting, stir to combine, and add the cream sauce, peas, and cheddar. Allow to simmer until warmed through, about 3 minutes. Top with the bread crumbs and serve.

SOY BROWN SUGAR–GLAZED SALMON

If you know people who are picky when it comes to the taste of fish, salmon may not be their favorite type of seafood. This recipe will help them to love salmon—the sweet and salty glaze, with the richness of the salmon, is sure to be a mealtime winner. Try serving underneath a salad or with white rice.

Prep time: 2 minutes | Cook time: 6 minutes (frozen) or 3 minutes (fresh) (MANUAL) + 4 minutes (SAUTÉ) | Serves 4

PRIMARY INGREDIENTS
¼ cup low-sodium soy sauce
3 tablespoons light brown sugar
Zest and juice of 1 lime
Four 6-ounce frozen or fresh center-cut
    salmon fillets, skin-on

ON-HAND INGREDIENTS
⅓ cup water
1 teaspoon freshly ground black pepper

TO SERVE
Salad or cooked rice

Whisk together the soy sauce, brown sugar, lime zest and juice, and ⅓ cup water in the bottom of the pressure cooker. Season with the pepper. Add the salmon fillets, skin-side up, secure the lid, and place on MANUAL with high pressure for 6 minutes for frozen salmon, or MANUAL with low pressure for 3 minutes for fresh. Quick release and remove the lid. Transfer the salmon to a plate. Select the SAUTÉ setting and reduce the sauce until glazelike, about 4 minutes, then pour over the top of the salmon fillets. Serve with salad or rice.

BEEF & PORK

BEEF STROGANOFF

When I was growing up in Ohio, this was a classic wintertime Midwestern dish and also my dad's favorite. Here is a quick, one-pot recipe that even impressed my dad.

Prep time: 5 minutes | Cook time: 11 minutes (SAUTÉ) + 18 minutes (MANUAL) + 4 minutes (SAUTÉ) | Serves 4

PRIMARY INGREDIENTS
1½ pounds beef chuck roast, cut into 1-inch pieces
1 cup frozen chopped onion, or 1 small onion, chopped
2½ cups thinly sliced cremini mushrooms
2 teaspoons herbes de Provence
1 cup unsalted beef stock
1 cup canned cream of mushroom soup, Cream Sauce (page 165), or store-bought cream sauce

ON-HAND INGREDIENTS
2 tablespoons olive oil
2 teaspoons kosher salt
1 teaspoon freshly ground black pepper

TO SERVE
1 pound egg noodles, cooked

Select the SAUTÉ setting and heat the olive oil. Season the beef with the salt and pepper and place in the pressure cooker—in batches if necessary. Allow to cook until browned on all sides, 6 to 7 minutes. Add the onion, mushrooms, and herbes de Provence and cook for another 5 minutes. Add the beef stock, secure the lid, and cook on MANUAL with high pressure for 18 minutes. Allow to naturally release for 5 minutes, then quick release and remove the lid. Select the SAUTÉ setting again and bring to a simmer. Stir in the cream of mushroom soup, ensuring there are no lumps, and allow to simmer until thickened, about 4 minutes. Serve over cooked egg noodles.

PULLED PORK SANDWICHES

Pulled pork sammies remind me of summer BBQs and fun times with friends. But pulled pork can often take forever to make. With this recipe, you'll have your summer party ready in about an hour.

Prep time: 5 minutes | Cook time: 10 minutes (SAUTÉ) + 55 minutes (MANUAL)
Serves 6 to 8

PRIMARY INGREDIENTS
One 3- to 4-pound boneless pork shoulder, cut into 4 pieces
1 cup chicken stock
1½ cups BBQ Sauce (page 161), or store-bought BBQ sauce

ON-HAND INGREDIENTS
1 tablespoon kosher salt
1 teaspoon freshly ground black pepper
2 tablespoons Cajun Spice Mix (page 154), or store-bought equivalent
2 tablespoons olive oil

TO SERVE
6 to 8 potato buns or kaiser rolls
Dill pickle chips

Sprinkle the pork shoulder on all sides with the salt, pepper, and Cajun spice mix. Select the SAUTÉ setting and heat the olive oil in the pressure cooker. Add the pork shoulder to the pot and sear on all sides, 10 to 12 minutes. Add the chicken stock, secure the lid, and cook on MANUAL with high pressure for 55 minutes. Allow to naturally release for 5 minutes, then quick release and remove the lid. Shred the pork, using two forks. Add the BBQ sauce and stir to combine, or serve on the side if preferred. Serve the pork on buns and with pickle chips.

CHEESY BACON POTATO CASSEROLE

Not only would I eat this dish for dinner, but it is also perfect for breakfast or lunch! During a busy week, you can make this casserole in advance, store in the fridge, and pressure cook right before you want to eat.

Prep time: 5 minutes | Cook time: 8 minutes (SAUTÉ) + 6 minutes (MANUAL) | Serves 4

PRIMARY INGREDIENTS

6 bacon strips, chopped
½ bunch scallions, chopped
Half of one 30-ounce bag frozen hash brown potatoes, thawed
1 cup shredded cheddar, plus more to sprinkle on top
1½ cups Cream Sauce (page 165), or store-bought cream sauce

ON-HAND INGREDIENTS

2 teaspoons kosher salt
½ teaspoon freshly ground black pepper
1 cup water

Select the SAUTÉ setting and place the bacon in the pressure cooker. Allow to cook until browned, about 6 minutes. Transfer to a paper towel–lined plate. Pour out all but 2 tablespoons of the bacon fat. Add the scallions to the pressure cooker and cook until tender, about 2 minutes. Wipe out the inner pot of the pressure cooker. Transfer the scallions to a large bowl and add the bacon and all the remaining ingredients, except the water and extra cheese, to the scallions. Mix to combine and transfer to a 7-cup heatproof glass baking dish or smaller insert and sprinkle the additional cheese on top. Place the steamer rack inside the pressure cooker and add 1 cup water. Place the baking dish on top of the steamer rack, cover with foil, secure the lid, and place on MANUAL with high pressure for 6 minutes. Allow to naturally release for 5 minutes, then quick release and remove the lid. Serve.

CLASSIC MEAT LOAF

I never thought meat loaf would be possible to make inside a pressure cooker or taste as good. I was wrong—this recipe is a delicious classic and still perfect to use in a sandwich as leftovers the next day.

Prep time: 8 minutes | Cook time: 40 minutes (MANUAL) | Serves 4

PRIMARY INGREDIENTS

1 pound lean ground beef

1 large egg

ON-HAND INGREDIENTS

1 tablespoon Italian Spice Mix (page 155), or store-bought equivalent

½ cup Herbed Bread Crumbs (page 158), or store-bought herbed bread crumbs

2 teaspoons kosher salt

1 teaspoon freshly ground black pepper

1 cup water

Cooking spray

TO SERVE

½ cup ketchup

Combine all the ingredients, except the ketchup, 1 cup water, and cooking spray, in a large bowl. Place the steamer rack inside the pressure cooker and add the water. Spray a 7-cup heatproof glass baking dish with cooking spray. Form the meat mixture into a circular shape and place in the baking dish. Cover the dish with foil and place on the steamer rack. Secure the lid and place on MANUAL with high pressure for 40 minutes. Allow to naturally release for 10 minutes, then quick release and remove the lid. Allow to cool for 5 minutes. Spread the ketchup over the top of the meat loaf, slice, and serve.

RED WINE BEEF SHORT RIBS

Beef short ribs are my usual go-to recipe when I am hosting a wintertime dinner party. My usual recipe takes over a day to make, which means a lot of advance planning. With this recipe, I can now plan to have short ribs on a Tuesday if I wanted—so crazy! Try serving with store-bought mashed potatoes.

Prep time: 5 minutes | Cook time: 12 minutes (SAUTÉ) + 38 minutes (MANUAL) | Serves 4

PRIMARY INGREDIENTS
3 pounds bone-in beef short ribs
1⅓ cups prechopped mixed onion, carrot, and celery
4 garlic cloves, minced, or 2 teaspoons jarred minced garlic
1 tablespoon tomato paste
1⅓ cups beef stock

ON-HAND INGREDIENTS
2 tablespoons olive oil
2 teaspoons kosher salt
1 teaspoon freshly ground black pepper

Select the SAUTÉ setting and heat the olive oil in the pressure cooker. Season the beef with the salt and pepper. Add the beef to the pot—in batches if necessary—and sear on all sides until browned, 7 to 9 minutes. Transfer from the pressure cooker to a plate. Add the vegetables to the pressure cooker and allow to cook until the onion is translucent, about 5 minutes, adding the garlic and tomato paste during the last minute of cooking. Deglaze the pan with the stock. Secure the lid and place on MANUAL with high pressure for 38 minutes. Allow to naturally release for 5 minutes, then quick release and remove the lid. Place back on SAUTÉ and allow the sauce to reduce until thickened, if necessary. Season with additional salt and pepper.

EASY POT ROAST WITH SMASHED POTATOES

Pot roast is always what my grandmother would serve if we went to her house in the wintertime. The delicious, homey smell of the roast with vegetables would drift through the whole house. This recipe brings me memories of her classic pot roast dinner.

Prep time: 5 minutes | Cook time: 11 minutes (SAUTÉ) + 60 minutes (MANUAL) | Serves 4

PRIMARY INGREDIENTS

One 3-pound boneless chuck roast, trimmed
1 yellow onion, thinly sliced
1¼ cups beef stock
1 pound baby Yukon Gold potatoes
3 carrots, peeled and cut into 3-inch pieces
2 tablespoons unsalted butter

ON-HAND INGREDIENTS

2 tablespoons olive oil
2 teaspoons kosher salt
1 teaspoon freshly ground black pepper
1 tablespoon dried thyme

Select the SAUTÉ setting and heat the olive oil in the pressure cooker. Season the chuck roast with the salt and pepper. Add the beef to the pot and sear on all sides until browned, about 7 minutes. Transfer the beef to a plate and set aside. Add the onion and thyme to the pressure cooker and cook for 4 minutes. Deglaze the pan with the beef stock. Add the chuck roast back to the pot, place the steamer rack on top, and place the potatoes and carrots on top of the steamer rack. Secure the lid and place on MANUAL with high pressure for 60 minutes. Allow to naturally release for 5 minutes, then quick release and remove the lid. Smash the potatoes with the back of a fork and season with additional salt and pepper. Remove the chuck roast and thinly slice or shred into large pieces, using two forks. Stir the butter into sauce. Serve over potatoes with sauce on top.

LEMON HERB PORK CHOPS

In elementary school, I would only eat pork chops with applesauce.
My pork chop palate has come a long way since then, such as with this
delicious lemon-herb recipe.

Prep time: 5 minutes | Cook time: 9 minutes (SAUTÉ) + 12 minutes (MANUAL) | Serves 4

PRIMARY INGREDIENTS
4 center-cut, bone-in pork chops
1 shallot, cut into small dice
2 garlic cloves, minced, or 1 teaspoon
    jarred minced garlic
⅔ cup chicken stock
¾ pound red-skin potatoes, cut in half
    if large

ON-HAND INGREDIENTS
2 tablespoons olive oil
2 teaspoons Lemon Herb Spice Mix
    (page 157), or store-bought equivalent
1 tablespoon kosher salt
1 teaspoon freshly ground black pepper

Select the SAUTÉ setting and heat the olive oil in the pressure cooker. Season the pork chops on both sides with the lemon herb spice mix, and half of the salt and pepper. Place the chops in the pot and sear on both sides until golden brown, about 4 minutes per side. Transfer the chops to a plate. You may need to sear them in batches. Add the shallot and garlic to the pressure cooker and cook for another minute. Add the chicken stock, scraping the browned bits up from the bottom of the pressure cooker. Return the pork chops to the pressure cooker, place a steamer rack on top, and add the red-skin potatoes. Season the potatoes with the remaining salt and pepper. Secure the lid and place on MANUAL with high pressure for 12 minutes. Allow to naturally release for 5 minutes, then quick release and remove the lid.

Note: Try cooking boneless frozen pork chops on MANUAL with high pressure for 15 minutes, or until cooked through and a meat thermometer registers 145°F.

CAJUN BBQ RIBS

Disappointed when you can't grill in the winter? Don't worry anymore! With this baby back rib recipe, you will get all that delicious summer flavor in the winter, and in half of the time.

Prep time: 5 minutes | Cook time: 25 minutes (MANUAL) | Serves 4

PRIMARY INGREDIENTS
One 4-pound rack baby back ribs
2 cups BBQ Sauce (page 161), or favorite
store-bought BBQ sauce, warmed

ON-HAND INGREDIENTS
1 cup water
2 tablespoons Cajun Spice Mix
(page 154), or store-bought equivalent
1 tablespoon kosher salt
2 teaspoons freshly ground black pepper

Remove the membrane on the back of the baby back ribs. Cut the ribs into three or four pieces. Place the steamer rack in the bottom of the pressure cooker and add 1 cup water. Sprinkle the ribs on both sides with the Cajun spice rub, salt, and pepper. Place the ribs on top of the steamer rack. Secure the lid and place on MANUAL with high pressure for 25 minutes. Allow to naturally release for 5 minutes, then quick release and remove the lid.

Remove the ribs from the pressure cooker and brush on both sides with the BBQ sauce or serve on the side. If desired, after brushing the ribs with the BBQ sauce, finish them under the broiler for 2 to 3 minutes for a nice glazed finish.

LEMON HERB PORK TENDERLOIN WITH APPLES AND ONIONS

Nothing says "busy weeknight meal" more than a pork tenderloin. What is great about pork tenderloin is that it is a canvas to try with so many flavors. This recipe's sweet and savory combination of flavors creates a dish that is so delicious.

Prep time: 10 minutes | Cook time: 12 minutes (SAUTÉ) + 12 minutes (MANUAL) | Serves 4

PRIMARY INGREDIENTS

1 pork tenderloin, trimmed, cut in half widthwise
2 yellow onions, thinly sliced
2 Honeycrisp apples, cored, cut into ¼-inch-thick slices
½ cup chicken stock
2 tablespoons Dijon mustard

ON-HAND INGREDIENTS

2 tablespoons olive oil
1 tablespoon Lemon Herb Spice Mix (page 157), or store-bought equivalent
2 teaspoons kosher salt
½ teaspoon freshly ground black pepper

Select the SAUTÉ setting and heat the olive oil in the pressure cooker. Season the pork tenderloin with the lemon herb spice mix, salt, and pepper. Place the tenderloin in the pot and sear on all sides until golden brown, 6 to 8 minutes. Transfer to a plate. Add the onions and apples to the pressure cooker and cook until lightly browned, another 6 minutes. Add the chicken stock and add back the pork. Secure the lid and set on MANUAL with high pressure for 12 minutes. Allow to naturally release for 5 minutes, then quick release and remove the lid. Remove the pork tenderloin from the pot and slice. Stir the Dijon mustard into the apple and onion mixture and serve on the side.

GREEN EGGS AND HAM POTATO CASSEROLE

This recipe is a great way to disguise vegetables for kids. I remember eating something similar during Dr. Seuss library class in elementary school and no one had a clue there was so much spinach!

Prep time: 10 minutes | Cook time: 25 minutes (MANUAL) | Serves 4

PRIMARY INGREDIENTS

⅔ cup heavy cream
2 large eggs, beaten
2 medium russet potatoes, peeled, sliced
    ¼-inch thick
One 10-ounce package frozen spinach,
    thawed and squeezed of excess liquid
½ ham steak, cut into ¼-inch cubes
1½ cups shredded white cheddar

ON-HAND INGREDIENTS

1½ cups water
Cooking spray
2 teaspoons Greek Spice Mix (page 153),
    or store-bought equivalent
2 teaspoons kosher salt
½ teaspoon freshly ground black pepper

Place the steamer rack in the bottom of the pressure cooker and add 1½ cups water. Grease a 7-cup heatproof glass baking dish with cooking spray. Combine the cream and eggs and season with Greek spice mix, salt, and pepper in a separate bowl. Layer the potatoes, spinach, cubed ham, and cheddar in alternating layers in the prepared baking dish, ending with the cheese. Pour the cream mixture over the top. Cover with foil and place in the pressure cooker. Secure the lid and set on MANUAL with high pressure for 25 minutes. Allow to naturally release for 5 minutes, then quick release and remove the lid. Allow to cool for 10 minutes, then serve.

Tip: Finish the bake under the oven broiler for a golden-brown finish!

SPAGHETTI SQUASH CARBONARA BOATS

When I was a kid, my mom transformed my view of spaghetti squash, to see it as a healthier alternative to pasta. The following recipe is just one example of how spaghetti squash can be reimagined in so many delicious ways.

Prep time: 5 minutes | Cook time: 7 minutes (SAUTÉ) + 8 minutes (MANUAL) | Serves 4

PRIMARY INGREDIENTS
5 bacon strips
1 spaghetti squash, cut in half lengthwise, seeds removed
1½ teaspoons garlic powder
1 teaspoon fresh thyme leaves, or 2 teaspoons dried
¾ to 1 cup grated Parmesan cheese, depending on the size of the squash

ON-HAND INGREDIENTS
2 tablespoons olive oil
1 cup water
2 teaspoons kosher salt
1 teaspoon freshly ground black pepper

TO SERVE
½ bunch scallions, thinly sliced, for garnish

Select the SAUTÉ setting and heat 1 tablespoon of the olive oil in the pressure cooker. Add the bacon and cook until crispy, about 7 minutes. Transfer to a paper towel–lined plate. Once cool, tear the bacon into smaller pieces. Drain the bacon fat from the pressure cooker.

Add the steamer rack and 1 cup water to the pressure cooker. Drizzle both halves of the spaghetti squash with the remaining tablespoon of olive oil. Season with the salt, pepper, garlic powder, and thyme. Place, cut side up, on the steamer rack. Secure the lid and place on MANUAL with high pressure for 8 minutes. Quick release and remove the lid. Remove the squash halves and carefully fluff the squash noodles into a large bowl, using a fork, reserving the squash skins for serving. Add the Parmesan cheese and bacon pieces to the squash noodles and stir until the cheese is melted. Serve the cheesy noodles in the reserved squash skins, garnished with the scallions.

TORTELLINI CASSEROLE WITH CORN AND BACON

The perfect summer pasta dish for a crowd! Use your favorite summer produce in this casserole for a fresh, seasonal meal.

Prep time: 5 minutes | Cook time: 8 minutes (SAUTÉ) + 3 minutes (MANUAL) | Serves 4

PRIMARY INGREDIENTS

5 bacon strips
One 10-ounce bag frozen corn, or
   1¼ cups fresh corn, cut off the cob
One 16-ounce package frozen tortellini
2 cups Tomato Sauce (page 162), or
   store-bought tomato sauce
1 cup shredded mozzarella

ON-HAND INGREDIENTS

1 tablespoon olive oil
2 teaspoons kosher salt
½ teaspoons freshly ground black pepper
½ cup water

TO SERVE

Fresh basil leaves, torn, for garnish

Select the SAUTÉ setting and heat the olive oil in the pressure cooker. Add the bacon and cook until crisp on both sides, about 7 minutes. Transfer to a paper towel–lined plate. When cool enough to touch, break into smaller pieces.

Drain all but 1 tablespoon of fat from the pressure cooker. Add the corn and cook for 1 minute. Season with the salt and pepper. Add ½ cup water, the tortellini, and the tomato sauce and do not stir. Secure the lid and cook on MANUAL with high pressure for 3 minutes. Quick release and remove the lid. Stir in the mozzarella cheese until melted and garnish with the bacon pieces and basil.

ONE-POT FAJITA PIE

Imagine a shepherd's pie, but fajita-style! This perfect combination of spice and cheese all in one pot is the perfect weeknight dinner solution. Use your favorite ground meat in this casserole!

Prep time: 2 minutes | Cook time: 13 minutes (SAUTÉ) + 7 minutes (MANUAL) | Serves 4

PRIMARY INGREDIENTS
1 pound ground beef (80/20)
1 red onion, small dice
One 15-ounce can black beans, drained and rinsed
One 10-ounce can red enchilada sauce
Four 6-inch corn tortillas
1 cup Mexican shredded cheese blend

ON-HAND INGREDIENTS
2 tablespoons olive oil
1 tablespoon plus 2 teaspoons Mexican Spice Mix (page 152), or store-bought equivalent
2 teaspoons kosher salt
½ teaspoon freshly ground black pepper
1 cup water

Select the SAUTÉ setting and heat the olive oil in the pressure cooker. Add the ground beef and cook until browned, 8 minutes, breaking it up with the back of a wooden spoon. Add the red onion and cook until tender, about 4 minutes. Add the Mexican spice mix, salt, pepper, and black beans and cook for another minute. Remove the beef mixture from the pressure cooker. Wipe out the pressure cooker using a paper towel and add 1 cup water and steamer rack. Place half of the beef mixture in a 7-cup glass dish. Add half of the enchilada sauce, two tortillas, and half of the cheese. Repeat one more time, ending with the cheese. Place the glass dish on the steamer rack, cover with foil, secure the lid, and cook on MANUAL with high pressure for 7 minutes. Allow to naturally release for 5 minutes, then quick release and remove the lid.

BEEF GOULASH

After a cold winter day, I always want to eat something hearty and delicious, such as this goulash. Try making this classic stewed beef dish with your favorite root vegetables.

Prep time: 5 minutes | Cook time: 12 minutes (SAUTÉ) + 12 minutes (MANUAL) + 3 minutes (SAUTÉ) | Serves 4

PRIMARY INGREDIENTS

2 pounds beef chuck roast, cut into
   1-inch pieces
1 cup chopped mixed carrot, celery,
   and onion
1 pound baby Yukon gold potatoes,
   cut in half if large
One 15-ounce can diced tomatoes
1 cup beef stock
One 16-ounce bag wide egg noodles

ON-HAND INGREDIENTS

2 tablespoons olive oil
2 teaspoons kosher salt
1 teaspoon freshly ground black pepper
5 teaspoons sweet paprika

Select the SAUTÉ setting and heat the olive oil in the pressure cooker. Season the beef on all sides with half of the salt and pepper. Place the beef in the pot and allow to brown on all sides, 7 to 9 minutes. Transfer to a plate. Add the vegetable mixture and cook until softened, about 4 minutes. Season with the remaining salt and pepper and add the paprika and potatoes. Cook for an additional minute. Add the tomatoes and beef stock, secure the lid, and cook on MANUAL with high pressure for 12 minutes. Quick release and remove the lid. Select the SAUTÉ setting and bring to a simmer, add the egg noodles and stir until tender, about 3 minutes. Serve.

SAUSAGE RAGU WITH POLENTA

Sausage ragu is one of my favorite things, whether it is with pasta or polenta. While this recipe uses sweet Italian sausage, I also like using hot Italian sausage for an extra-spicy kick.

Prep time: 5 minutes | Cook time: 12 minutes (SAUTÉ) + 10 minutes (MANUAL) | Serves 4

PRIMARY INGREDIENTS

1 pound sweet Italian sausage, removed from casings
1 cup chopped mixed carrot, celery, and onion
4 garlic cloves, minced, or 2 teaspoons jarred minced garlic
1 cup polenta
One 28-ounce can crushed San Marzano tomatoes

ON-HAND INGREDIENTS

2 tablespoons olive oil
2 teaspoons kosher salt
1 teaspoon freshly ground black pepper
2½ teaspoons Italian Spice Mix (page 155), or store-bought equivalent
1½ cups water

TO SERVE

Grated Parmesan cheese, for garnish

Select the SAUTÉ setting and heat the olive oil in the pressure cooker. Add the sausage and cook until browned, breaking it up into crumbles, using the back of a wooden spoon, 7 to 9 minutes. Season with half of the salt and pepper. Add the vegetable mixture and cook until softened, about 4 minutes. Season with the remaining salt and pepper. Add the garlic and Italian spice mix and cook for an additional minute. Add 1½ cups water, polenta, and tomatoes and do not stir! Secure the lid and cook on MANUAL with high pressure for 10 minutes. Quick release and remove the lid. Stir to combine and serve garnished with Parmesan.

EASY FRENCH DIP SANDWICHES

French dip sandwiches are something I usually wouldn't think to make at home, but discovered that the pressure cooker makes it so easy. Be sure to save the broth in this recipe for the best sandwich-dunking experience!

Prep time: 5 minutes | Cook time: 15 minutes (SAUTÉ) + 40 minutes (MANUAL)
Serves 4 to 6

PRIMARY INGREDIENTS
One 3-pound boneless beef chuck roast
2 yellow onions, thinly sliced
1 teaspoon fresh thyme leaves, or
   2 teaspoons dried
3 garlic cloves, minced, or 1½ teaspoons
   jarred minced garlic
1 cup low-sodium beef broth

ON-HAND INGREDIENTS
2 tablespoons olive oil
2 teaspoons kosher salt
1 teaspoon freshly ground black pepper
2 tablespoons butter

TO SERVE
4 to 6 baguettes, cut into 6-inch buns,
   toasted
12 to 18 slices provolone

Select the SAUTÉ setting and heat the olive oil in the pressure cooker. Season the chuck roast on both sides with the salt and pepper. Add the beef to the pot and cook until a deep golden brown on both sides, 7 to 9 minutes. Transfer to a plate. Add the onions to the pressure cooker and cook until golden brown, 8 to 10 minutes (you can add a pinch of sugar to help speed up this process!), adding the thyme and garlic during the last minute of cooking. Deglaze the pot with the beef broth, scraping any browned bits from the bottom of the pan. Return the chuck roast to the pot, secure the lid, and place on MANUAL with high pressure for 40 minutes. Allow to naturally release for 5 minutes, then quick release and remove the lid. Remove the roast, allow to rest for 10 minutes, then thinly slice the meat. Place on the toasted buns and top each with 3 slices of cheese. Serve with the onion broth on the side in separate bowls.

SAUSAGE AND CHEESE BREAD PUDDING

Breakfast becomes my favorite meal of the day when something hearty and savory is served, such as this bread pudding. Better yet, I would even serve this dish as breakfast for dinner! Try using your favorite breakfast meats and cheeses in this recipe.

Prep time: 8 minutes | Cook time: 7 minutes (SAUTÉ) + 10 minutes (MANUAL) | Serves 4

PRIMARY INGREDIENTS
¾ pound sweet Italian sausage, removed from casings
½ red onion, cut into small dice
¾ cup shredded cheddar
3 cups day-old sourdough or white bread, cut into 1-inch cubes
4 large eggs
¾ cup whole milk

ON-HAND INGREDIENTS
1 tablespoon olive oil
2 teaspoons Cajun Spice Mix (page 154), or store-bought equivalent
2 teaspoons kosher salt
1 teaspoon freshly ground black pepper
Cooking spray
1 cup water

Select the SAUTÉ setting and heat the olive oil in the pressure cooker. Add the sausage to the pot and cook until browned, 7 to 9 minutes, breaking it into crumbles, using the back of a wooden spoon. Add the onion during the last 4 minutes of cooking, sautéing until the onion is softened. Season with Cajun spice mix and half of the salt and pepper. Spray a 7-cup heatproof glass baking dish or 6-inch cake pan with cooking spray. Transfer the sausage to the dish and top with the cheese and bread cubes. Whisk the eggs, whole milk, and remaining salt and pepper together in a large bowl. Pour over the bread cubes and press down on the bread to ensure that is has soaked through. Wipe out the pot using a paper towel.

Place the steamer rack inside the pressure cooker and add 1 cup water. Cover the bread pudding with a piece of paper towel and then foil and place on the steamer rack. Secure the lid and place on MANUAL with high pressure for 10 minutes. Allow to naturally release for 10 minutes, then quick release and remove the lid. Serve.

SPAGHETTI AND MEAT SAUCE

As a kid, I always knew dinner was going to be great if it was spaghetti and meat sauce, a true classic. This version is so easy, the pasta even goes in the pressure cooker!

Prep time: 2 minutes | Cook time: 11 minutes (SAUTÉ) + 6 minutes (MANUAL) | Serves 4

PRIMARY INGREDIENTS
¾ pound ground beef (80/20)
1 yellow onion, small dice
3 garlic cloves, minced, or 1½ teaspoons jarred minced garlic
½ pound spaghetti, broken in half
One 28-ounce can crushed San Marzano tomatoes

ON-HAND INGREDIENTS
2 tablespoons olive oil
2 teaspoons kosher salt
1 teaspoon freshly ground black pepper
2 teaspoons Italian Spice Mix (page 155), or store-bought equivalent
1½ cups water

TO SERVE
Grated Parmesan

Select the SAUTÉ setting and heat the olive oil in the pressure cooker. Add the ground beef to the pot and cook until browned, breaking it up with the back of a wooden spoon, 7 to 9 minutes. Add the onion and cook until translucent, about 4 minutes. Season with the salt, pepper, and Italian spice mix, adding the garlic during the last minute of cooking. Add 1½ cups water, spaghetti, and crushed tomatoes (in that order and do not stir!). Secure the lid and place on MANUAL with high pressure for 6 minutes. Quick release and remove the lid. Serve with Parmesan cheese!

MUSHROOM AND BACON RISOTTO

When I asked my friends if they would make risotto at home, everyone thought I was crazy. When I had them taste this easy pressure cooker risotto and told them how long it took me to make, they didn't believe me. Now they are making their own versions of risotto every week in their pressure cookers—it's a dinnertime game-changer.

Prep time: 2 minutes | Cook time: 15 minutes (SAUTÉ) + 4 minutes (MANUAL) | Serves 4

PRIMARY INGREDIENTS
½ pound bacon, chopped
½ cup chopped yellow onion
Two 8-ounce packages sliced cremini
  mushrooms
1 teaspoon fresh thyme or 2 teaspoons
  dried thyme
1½ cups uncooked Arborio rice
¾ cup grated Parmesan, plus more for
  garnish

ON-HAND INGREDIENTS
1 tablespoon olive oil
2 teaspoons kosher salt
1 teaspoon freshly ground black pepper
3¼ cups water

Select the SAUTÉ setting and heat the olive oil in the pressure cooker. Add the bacon to the pot and cook until crisp, about 7 minutes. Transfer to a paper towel-lined plate and pour all but 2 tablespoons of bacon fat out of the pressure cooker insert. Add the onion and mushrooms and cook until browned, about 7 minutes. Season with the salt and pepper. Add the thyme and cook for an additional minute. Add the rice and stir to coat in the fat. Add 3¼ cups water, secure the lid, and cook on MANUAL with high pressure for 4 minutes. Quick release and remove the lid. Stir to combine and add the bacon to the pot along with the cheese. Allow the cheese to melt, then serve garnished with additional cheese.

SOUPS & STEWS

WHITE CHICKEN CHILI

Something I love about chili is how versatile it can become with almost no effort. I usually choose whatever vegetables, canned beans, and meat—whether sausage, shredded chicken, or ground meat—sounds good that day. Stew it all together in almost no time in your pressure cooker and it is the perfect dinner or lunchtime meal.

Prep time: 5 minutes | Cook time: 11 minutes (SAUTÉ) + 9 minutes (MANUAL) + 3 minutes (SAUTÉ) | Serves 4

PRIMARY INGREDIENTS

3 boneless, skinless chicken breasts,
  cut into 1-inch pieces
1 small red onion, cut into small dice
One 4.5-ounce can green chiles
4 cups chicken stock
Two 15-ounce cans cannellini beans,
  drained and rinsed
1 cup frozen corn

ON-HAND INGREDIENTS

2 tablespoons olive oil
2 teaspoons kosher salt
1 teaspoon freshly ground black pepper
1 tablespoon Mexican Spice Mix
  (page 152), or store-bought equivalent

Select the SAUTÉ setting and heat the olive oil in the pressure cooker. Season the chicken with the salt and pepper and sear on all sides until golden brown, about 6 minutes. Add the red onion and cook until almost tender, about 4 minutes. Add the Mexican spice mix and green chiles and cook for an additional minute. Add the chicken stock, secure the lid, and cook on MANUAL with high pressure for 9 minutes. Quick release and remove the lid. Select the SAUTÉ setting and bring to a simmer. Mash one can of beans in a small bowl, using a wooden spoon or fork. Whisk the mashed beans into the simmering soup. Add the remaining can of beans and the corn and simmer until warmed through, 3 to 4 minutes.

CHICKEN TORTILLA SOUP

Anytime my mom would make roast chicken for dinner when I was a kid, she would use the leftover carcass to make the most delicious chicken tortilla soup. This recipe is inspired by her recipe—try adding hot sauce or a little bit of cayenne pepper if you like it spicy!

Prep time: 5 minutes | Cook time: 7 minutes (SAUTÉ) + 10 minutes (MANUAL) | Serves 4

PRIMARY INGREDIENTS

1 small red onion, cut into small dice
1 rotisserie chicken, skin and bones
   removed and discarded, shredded
2 teaspoons ground cumin
Two 15-ounce cans diced tomatoes with
   garlic and chile
4 cups chicken stock

ON-HAND INGREDIENTS

1 tablespoon olive oil
2 teaspoons kosher salt
1 teaspoon freshly ground black pepper

TO SERVE

Tortilla strips, for garnish
Optional: crumbled queso fresco or
   shredded cheddar, sour cream, and
   avocado

Select the SAUTÉ setting and heat the olive oil in the pressure cooker. Add the onion and cook until tender, about 4 minutes. Add the shredded chicken and cumin and season with the salt and pepper. Cook for 3 minutes. Add the tomatoes and chicken stock, secure the lid, and cook on MANUAL with high pressure for 10 minutes. Quick release and remove the lid. Serve garnished with tortilla strips and any additional toppings.

BROCCOLI CHEDDAR SOUP

I always loved when it was broccoli cheddar soup day in the school cafeteria in elementary school. The creaminess of the soup with the little "green trees" and a big piece of crusty bread on the side—nothing could be more perfect at that moment. This recipe brings the comfort of classic Broccoli Cheddar Soup to your pressure cooker.

Prep time: 5 minutes | Cook time: 5 minutes (SAUTÉ) + 6 minutes (MANUAL) + 5 minutes (SAUTÉ) | Serves 4

PRIMARY INGREDIENTS

1 yellow onion, chopped, or 1 cup frozen chopped onion

½ teaspoon paprika

10 ounces fresh broccoli florets, or one 10- to 12-ounce bag frozen broccoli florets

2 cups chicken stock

1 cup Cream Sauce (page 165), or store-bought cream sauce

1½ cups grated sharp cheddar

ON-HAND INGREDIENTS

2 tablespoons olive oil

2 teaspoons kosher salt

½ teaspoon freshly ground black pepper

Select the SAUTÉ setting and heat the olive oil in the pressure cooker. Add the onion and cook until translucent, about 5 minutes. Add the paprika and season with the salt and pepper. Add the broccoli and chicken stock. Secure the lid and place on MANUAL with high pressure for 6 minutes. Quick release and remove the lid. Select the SAUTÉ setting and bring to a simmer. Stir in the cream sauce and cheddar and allow to warm through and the cheese to melt, about 5 minutes. Serve.

TURKEY CHILI

During the wintertime, turkey chili is definitely my go-to meal. It is simple to make for the week on a Sunday night and even better two days later. I love serving it over a baked potato, penne pasta, or even spaghetti squash. This recipe is so simple, but flavorful and delicious—make a couple of batches in advance and freeze for an easy weeknight meal.

Prep time: 2 minutes | Cook time: 11 minutes (SAUTÉ) +12 minutes (MANUAL) + 4 minutes (SAUTÉ) | Serves 4

PRIMARY INGREDIENTS
1 pound ground turkey meat
1½ cups chopped mixed onion and bell peppers or frozen mixed onion and bell peppers
¼ cup chili powder
Two 15-ounce cans diced tomatoes with garlic
Two 15-ounce cans red kidney beans, drained and rinsed

ON-HAND INGREDIENTS
2 tablespoons olive oil
2 teaspoons kosher salt
1 teaspoon freshly ground black pepper
2½ cups water

TO SERVE
Shredded sharp cheddar, for garnish
Scallions, for garnish (optional)

Select the SAUTÉ setting and heat the olive oil in the pressure cooker. Add the turkey and brown, breaking up with the back of a wooden spoon, until golden, about 7 minutes. Season with the salt and pepper. Add the onion and bell pepper mixture and cook for another 4 minutes. Add the chili powder and cook another minute. Add the tomatoes and 2½ cupswater, secure the lid, and cook on MANUAL with high pressure for 12 minutes. Quick release and remove the lid. Select the SAUTÉ setting and bring to a simmer. Add the beans and allow to warm through, about 4 minutes. Serve the chili garnished with shredded cheddar and scallions, if using.

LEMON CAULIFLOWER POTATO SOUP

Cauliflower is a wonderful vegetable because once boiled and mashed or pureed, it can become so creamy, you would think it had added cream! This fresh yet hearty soup could be served as a starter or side or a main course.

Prep time: 3 minutes | Cook time: 8 minutes (SAUTÉ) + 7 minutes (MANUAL) | Serves 4

PRIMARY INGREDIENTS

14 ounces fresh cauliflower florets (about 4 cups), or one 14-ounce bag frozen cauliflower florets
1 shallot, cut into small dice
2 garlic cloves, minced, or 1 teaspoon jarred minced garlic
2 Yukon gold potatoes, peeled and cut into 1-inch dice
2 cups vegetable stock
2 tablespoons fresh lemon juice

ON-HAND INGREDIENTS

2 tablespoons olive oil
2 teaspoons kosher salt
1 teaspoon freshly ground black pepper

Select the SAUTÉ setting and heat the olive oil in the pressure cooker. Add the cauliflower florets and cook until golden brown, about 7 minutes. Add the shallot and garlic and sauté for an additional minute. Season with the salt and pepper. Add the potatoes and vegetable stock, secure the lid, and set on MANUAL with high pressure for 7 minutes. Quick release and remove the lid. Mash the cauliflower and potato until smooth, using a potato masher or fork. Stir in the lemon juice and serve.

CAJUN CORN CHOWDER

While I was growing up in Ohio, when the summer corn came into season, we would eat it raw off the cob—the corn is that sweet and delicious on its own. This corn chowder makes the sweet deliciousness of corn shine, whether it is fresh off the cob or frozen.

Prep time: 5 minutes | Cook time: 15 minutes (SAUTÉ) + 6 minutes (MANUAL) + 3 minutes (SAUTÉ) | Serves 4

PRIMARY INGREDIENTS
5 bacon strips
1 small yellow onion, small dice
4 cups corn kernels, cut off cob, or frozen corn kernels
2 cups chicken stock
¾ cup Cream Sauce (page 165), or ⅔ cup heavy cream

ON-HAND INGREDIENTS
1 tablespoon olive oil
1½ teaspoons Cajun Spice Mix (page 154), or store-bought equivalent
2 teaspoons kosher salt
1 teaspoon freshly ground black pepper

TO SERVE
Whole-grain tortilla chips (optional)

Select the SAUTÉ setting and heat the olive oil in the pressure cooker. Add the bacon and cook until crispy and browned, about 7 minutes. Transfer to a paper towel–lined plate. Once cooled, break into tiny pieces and set aside.

Remove all but 2 tablespoons of bacon grease from the pressure cooker. Add the onion to the pressure cooker and cook until translucent, about 4 minutes. Add the Cajun spice mix, salt, and pepper and allow to cook for an additional minute. Add the corn and cook for another 3 minutes. Add the chicken stock, secure the lid, and set on MANUAL with high pressure for 6 minutes. Quick release, remove the lid, and select the SAUTÉ setting. Stir in the cream sauce and allow to simmer until slightly thickened, about 3 minutes. Serve with whole-grain tortilla chips.

BEEF AND BARLEY STEW

This classic stew was always my great-grandfather's favorite wintertime soup to order at a diner or café with his Reuben sandwich. This recipe makes the stew simple with just six ingredients!

Prep time: 2 minutes | Cook time: 12 minutes (SAUTÉ) + 18 minutes (MANUAL) + 6 minutes (SAUTÉ) | Serves 4

PRIMARY INGREDIENTS

1 pound beef chuck roast, cut into 1-inch pieces
1 yellow onion, cut into small dice
1 cup pearled barley
2 cups beef stock
One 15-ounce can diced tomatoes
One 10-ounce bag frozen mixed potato and vegetables

ON-HAND INGREDIENTS

2 tablespoons olive oil
2 teaspoons kosher salt
1 teaspoon freshly ground black pepper
1 tablespoon Greek Spice Mix (page 153), or store-bought equivalent

Select the SAUTÉ setting and heat the olive oil in the pressure cooker. Season the beef on all sides with the salt and pepper. Sear the beef on all sides until browned, about 7 minutes. Transfer to a plate. Add the onion and cook until translucent, about 4 minutes. Add the Greek spice mix and cook for an additional minute. Add the barley, beef stock, diced tomatoes, and browned beef. Secure the lid and place on MANUAL with high pressure for 18 minutes. Allow to naturally release for 5 minutes, then quick release and remove the lid. Select the SAUTÉ setting and bring to a simmer. Add the potato and vegetable mixture and allow to simmer until cooked through, another 6 to 7 minutes. Serve.

PLANT-BASED MEALS

BUTTERNUT SQUASH RISOTTO

When fall comes around and butternut squash and pumpkin are in season, this is a dish that I instantly crave but usually don't have hours to make— that problem is solved with the pressure cooker.

Prep time: 2 minutes | Cook time: 10 minutes (SAUTÉ) + 4 minutes (MANUAL) | Serves 4

PRIMARY INGREDIENTS

4 tablespoons unsalted butter
½ cup chopped yellow onion
One 10-ounce bag frozen diced butternut squash, or 10 ounces diced fresh butternut squash
1½ cups Arborio rice
3¼ cups vegetable stock
¾ cup grated Parmesan, plus more for garnish

ON-HAND INGREDIENTS

1½ teaspoons dried thyme
2 teaspoons kosher salt
½ teaspoon freshly ground black pepper

Select the SAUTÉ setting and heat 2 tablespoons of the butter in the pressure cooker. Add the onion and cook until tender, about 4 minutes. Add the squash and cook until lightly browned, another 4 minutes. Add the thyme and season with the salt and pepper. Add the rice and allow to cook until the rice is coated in butter, about 2 minutes. Add the stock, secure the lid, and set on MANUAL with high pressure for 4 minutes. Quick release, then remove the lid and insert from the pressure cooker. Stir immediately to combine and add the cheese and remaining 2 tablespoons of butter and stir again. Serve with additional grated Parmesan on top.

MAC & CHEESE WITH CAULIFLOWER

Mac and cheese is something that I will never stop loving—what can't be good about noodles and cheese sauce? But sometimes, I am looking for a healthier version of mac and cheese and this is my go-to recipe. Using cauliflower, you really can't even tell that it isn't all noodles covered in that delicious, creamy sauce.

Prep time: 2 minutes | Cook time: 4 minutes (MANUAL) + 4 minutes (SAUTÉ) | Serves 4

PRIMARY INGREDIENTS

1 pound elbow pasta

2 cups fresh cauliflower florets or frozen

2 teaspoons Dijon mustard

¾ cup reduced-fat milk

6 ounces cream cheese, at room temperature

2 cups shredded cheddar

ON-HAND INGREDIENTS

3½ cups water

1 teaspoon kosher salt

2 teaspoons freshly ground black pepper

TO SERVE

1 cup Herbed Bread Crumbs (page 158), or store-bought herbed bread crumbs, for garnish (optional)

Place the pasta, cauliflower florets, and 3½ cups water in the bowl of the pressure cooker. Secure the lid and cook on MANUAL with high pressure for 4 minutes. Use quick release and remove the lid. Drain any additional water.

Select the SAUTÉ setting and add the remaining ingredients, except the bread crumbs. Stir until the cheese has melted and coated the pasta, about 4 minutes. Serve, garnished with herbed bread crumbs if desired.

CAPRESE PASTA BAKE

It's always exciting when summer comes around and the juicy, sweet tomatoes are just perfect to make a Caprese salad with fresh mozzarella and basil—I have to eat this salad at least once a week. This easy pasta bake helps you enjoy those flavors all year round.

Prep time: 2 minutes | Cook time: 5 minutes (SAUTÉ) + 5 minutes (MANUAL) | Serves 4

PRIMARY INGREDIENTS
1 yellow onion, cut into small dice
4 garlic cloves, minced, or 2 teaspoons jarred minced garlic
1 pound fusilli
One 15-ounce can diced tomatoes
2 cups Tomato Sauce (page 162), or store-bought tomato sauce
1½ cups shredded mixed mozzarella and Parmesan

ON-HAND INGREDIENTS
2 tablespoons olive oil
2 teaspoons kosher salt
2 teaspoons freshly ground black pepper
2½ teaspoons Italian Spice Mix (page 155), or store-bought equivalent
1½ cups water

Select the SAUTÉ setting and heat the olive oil. Add the onion and cook until translucent, about 4 minutes. Add the garlic, salt, pepper, and Italian spice mix and cook for an additional minute. Add the pasta, 1½ cups water, tomatoes, and tomato sauce (in that order!). Secure the lid and set on MANUAL with high pressure for 5 minutes. Quick release and remove the lid. Stir in the shredded cheese and allow to melt.

QUINOA-STUFFED BELL PEPPERS

Stuffed peppers are a classic that always had me wondering what delicious filling would be on the inside. I love using whole grains, such as quinoa, mixed with spices and veggies to make a substantial filling that is fresh and satisfying.

Prep time: 10 minutes | Cook time: 15 minutes (MANUAL) | Serves 4

PRIMARY INGREDIENTS
1½ cups frozen, precooked quinoa
1 cup frozen spinach, thawed and
  squeezed of excess liquid
⅓ cup store-bought pesto
1 cup cherry tomatoes, quartered
2 large red bell peppers, cut in half
  lengthwise, seeds removed
1 cup grated Parmesan

ON-HAND INGREDIENTS
1 cup water
2 teaspoons kosher salt
1 teaspoon freshly ground black pepper
2 teaspoons Greek Spice Mix (page 153),
  or store-bought equivalent

Place the steamer rack in the bowl of the pressure cooker and add 1 cup water. Combine the quinoa, spinach, pesto, tomatoes, salt, black pepper, and Greek spice mix in a large bowl. Divide among the bell pepper halves; they will be very full. Place the peppers, stuffing side up, on the steamer rack and top with the Parmesan. Secure the lid and place on MANUAL with high pressure for 15 minutes. Quick release and remove the lid.

EGGPLANT PARMESAN

On a weeknight after a long day of cooking and eating at work, nothing sounds better than picking up eggplant Parmesan takeout from my corner pizzeria in New York. But . . . to keep my wallet happy, I like to avoid takeout during the week. This is how this delicious recipe came to be, and I must say, I rarely miss my pizzeria's eggplant Parmesan.

Prep time: 20 minutes | Cook time: 12 minutes (MANUAL) | Serves 4

PRIMARY INGREDIENTS

1 large or 2 small eggplants, sliced into
   ¼-inch rings
2 cups Tomato Sauce (page 162), or
   store-bought tomato sauce
One 8-ounce ball fresh mozzarella
   drained, sliced into ¼-inch rounds

ON-HAND INGREDIENTS

1 cup water
¼ cup plus 2 teaspoons kosher salt
1 teaspoon freshly ground black pepper
2 tablespoons Italian Spice Mix
   (page 155), or store-bought equivalent

TO SERVE

1 cup Herbed Bread Crumbs (page 158),
   or store-bought herbed bread crumbs,
   for garnish
½ cup grated parmesan, for garnish
1 bunch basil, chopped, for garnish

Place the steamer rack into the bowl of the pressure cooker and add 1 cup water. Sprinkle the eggplant on both sides with the ¼ cup of salt and allow to sit for 10 minutes to remove some excess liquid. Rinse the eggplant and pat dry.

Pour a thin layer of tomato sauce into a 7-cup heatproof glass baking dish. Season the eggplant with the salt, pepper, and Italian spice mix. Layer the eggplant rounds on top of the sauce in an even layer and top with a layer of mozzarella. Ladle another layer of sauce on top of the mozzarella and continue to layer eggplant, mozzarella, and sauce until all the ingredients are used, ending with a final layer of sauce. Cover with foil, secure the lid, and cook on MANUAL with high pressure for 12 minutes. Allow to naturally release for 5 minutes, then quick release and remove the lid. Garnish with herbed bread crumbs, parmesan, and basil, and serve.

CHEESY SPINACH ALFREDO RAVIOLI "BAKE"

I love the idea of a ravioli bake because it is basically the sister to lasagna but a lot easier to make. This recipe is a take on a classic ravioli bake and uses herbed bread crumbs to achieve a crunchy golden-brown topping.

Prep time: 2 minutes | Cook time: 3 minutes (SAUTÉ) + 6 minutes (MANUAL) + 4 minutes (SAUTÉ) | Serves 4

PRIMARY INGREDIENTS

One 10-ounce package frozen spinach, thawed and squeezed of excess liquid
2 garlic cloves, minced, or 1 teaspoon jarred minced garlic
20 ounces frozen cheese ravioli
1 cup grated Parmesan
1½ cups Cream Sauce (page 165), or store-bought alfredo sauce

ON-HAND INGREDIENTS

2 tablespoons olive oil
2 teaspoons kosher salt
½ teaspoon freshly ground black pepper
2 cups water

TO SERVE

1 cup Herbed Bread Crumbs (page 158), or store-bought herbed bread crumbs, for garnish

Select the SAUTÉ setting and heat the olive oil in the pressure cooker. Add the spinach and cook for 3 minutes, adding the garlic during the last minute of cooking. Season with the salt and pepper. Add the ravioli and 2 cups water. Secure the lid and cook on MANUAL with high pressure for 6 minutes. Quick release and remove the lid. Drain any excess liquid. Return the pressure cooker to SAUTÉ setting and stir in the cream sauce and cheese until warmed through, about 4 minutes. Serve garnished with bread crumbs.

EGGS FLORENTINE STRATA

I don't know about you, but since I am cooking for just myself most of the time, my bread usually goes stale before I am finished with the loaf. To keep from throwing good bread away, I love to use my stale bread in something like this strata to make a flavorful dish that can be eaten for any meal of the day.

Prep time: 10 minutes | Cook time: 6 minutes (SAUTÉ) + 6 minutes (MANUAL) | Serves 4

PRIMARY INGREDIENTS

One 8-ounce package pre-sliced cremini mushrooms
One 10-ounce package frozen spinach, thawed and squeezed of excess liquid
5 cups 1-inch-cubed day-old bread
4 large eggs, beaten
1 cup shredded Parmesan
½ cup vegetable stock

ON-HAND INGREDIENTS

2 tablespoons olive oil
2 teaspoons kosher salt
½ teaspoon freshly ground black pepper
1 tablespoon Greek Spice Mix (page 153), or store-bought equivalent
1 cup water

Select the SAUTÉ setting and heat the olive oil in the pressure cooker. Add the mushrooms and cook until tender, about 5 minutes. Add the spinach and cook for an additional minute. Season with the salt, pepper, and Greek spice mix.

Combine the bread, eggs, Parmesan, spinach mixture, and mushrooms in a large bowl. Add the vegetable stock and mix to combine. Transfer to a 7-cup heatproof glass baking dish and cover with foil. Place the steamer rack inside the pressure cooker and add 1 cup water. Place the foil-covered baking dish on the steamer rack. Secure the lid and place on MANUAL with high pressure for 6 minutes. Quick release and remove the lid. Serve.

PUMPKIN SAGE PASTA

Canned pumpkin is one of those secret ingredients you should always have in your pantry. I love to use it in easy soups, casseroles, and pasta dishes, such as this one.

Prep time: 2 minutes | Cook time: 4 minutes (SAUTÉ) + 4 minutes (MANUAL) | Serves 4

PRIMARY INGREDIENTS

2 garlic cloves, minced, or 1 teaspoon jarred minced garlic
¼ teaspoon ground nutmeg
5 sage leaves
1 pound spaghetti, broken in half
One 15-ounce can pure pumpkin puree

ON-HAND INGREDIENTS

2 tablespoons olive oil
2 teaspoons kosher salt
½ teaspoon freshly ground black pepper
1½ cups water

TO SERVE

½ cup Herbed Bread Crumbs (page 158), or store-bought herbed bread crumbs, for garnish
½ cup grated Parmesan, for garnish

Select the SAUTÉ setting and heat the olive oil in the pressure cooker. Add the garlic, nutmeg, and sage and cook until the garlic is golden and the sage is crispy, about 4 minutes. Season with the salt and pepper. Add 1½ cups water, pasta, and pumpkin puree (in that order, do not stir!). Secure the lid and cook on MANUAL with high pressure for 4 minutes. Quick release and remove the lid. Stir to combine the pasta and sauce. Garnish with the herbed bread crumbs and grated Parmesan.

SOFT-BOILED EGGS IN SPICY TOMATO SAUCE

This is probably my favorite brunch recipe. Whether I am making it at home or ordering it at a restaurant, there is nothing like breaking open a soft egg in tomato sauce that is served with crusty bread for dipping. I prefer my sauce spicy, but leave out the cayenne if you prefer your sauce mild.

Prep time: 9 minutes | Cook time: 9 minutes (SAUTÉ) + 10 minutes (MANUAL) + 3 minutes (SAUTÉ) | Serves 4

PRIMARY INGREDIENTS
½ red onion, finely diced
2 garlic cloves, minced, or 1 teaspoon jarred minced garlic
1 green bell pepper, stem and seeds removed, small diced small
One 15-ounce can crushed tomatoes
4 large eggs

ON-HAND INGREDIENTS
2 tablespoons olive oil
1 teaspoon kosher salt
½ teaspoon freshly ground black pepper
2 teaspoons Mexican Spice Mix (page 152), or store-bought equivalent

TO SERVE
Crumbled feta cheese, for garnish (optional)
Toasted crusty bread

Select the SAUTÉ setting and heat the oil in the pressure cooker. Add the onion, garlic, and bell pepper and cook until the onion is translucent, about 6 minutes. Season with the salt, black pepper, and Mexican spice mix. Add the tomatoes and bring to a simmer, 3 to 4 minutes. Secure the lid of the pressure cooker and place on MANUAL with low pressure for 10 minutes. Allow to natural release for 5 minutes, then quick release and remove the lid.

Select SAUTÉ again on the pressure cooker and bring the sauce to a simmer. Drop the eggs in one by one, making pockets in the sauce, and allow to simmer until the whites are just cooked through but the yolk is still runny, 3 to 4 minutes. Serve garnished with feta cheese, if desired, and crusty bread.

RATATOUILLE

When summer comes around, and you overbuy vegetables at the farmers' market (at least I do!), this is the perfect dish to use all those summer veggies before they go bad.

Prep time: 10 minutes | Cook time: 13 minutes (SAUTÉ) + 4 minutes (MANUAL) | Serves 4

PRIMARY INGREDIENTS

1 eggplant, cut into ½-inch dice
2 zucchini, cut into ½-inch dice
2 yellow squash, cut into ½-inch dice
1 red bell pepper, cut into ½-inch dice
1 teaspoon fresh thyme leaves, or
   2 teaspoons dried thyme
1 cup cherry tomatoes, halved

ON-HAND INGREDIENTS

2 tablespoons olive oil
2 teaspoons kosher salt
1 teaspoon freshly ground black pepper
⅓ cup water

TO SERVE

½ cup Herbed Bread Crumbs (page 158), or store-bought herbed bread crumbs, for garnish

Select the SAUTÉ setting and heat the olive oil in the pressure cooker. Add the eggplant and cook until browned on all sides, 7 to 8 minutes. Season with the salt and pepper. Add the zucchini, yellow squash, and bell pepper and cook until lightly browned, about 5 minutes. Add the thyme and tomatoes and cook for an additional minute. Add ⅓ cup water, secure the lid, and place on MANUAL with high pressure for 4 minutes. Quick release and remove the lid. Serve, garnished with the herbed bread crumbs.

TUSCAN WHITE BEAN PASTA

One of my favorite weeknight meal options when I am in a pinch is a pantry pasta dish. This Tuscan White Bean Pasta is just that kind of recipe. Stock up on these staple ingredients on your next grocery store run, and you will be able to have a delicious meal on the table in minutes.

Prep time: 2 minutes | Cook time: 4 minutes (SAUTÉ) + 5 minutes (MANUAL) + 4 minutes (SAUTÉ) | Serves 4

PRIMARY INGREDIENTS
½ cup chopped fresh or frozen yellow onion
2 garlic cloves, minced, or 1 teaspoon jarred minced garlic
1½ cups Tomato Sauce (page 162), or store-bought pasta sauce
1 pound large elbow pasta
One 15-ounce can cannellini beans, drained and rinsed

ON-HAND INGREDIENTS
1 tablespoon olive oil
2 teaspoons kosher salt
1 teaspoon freshly ground black pepper
2 teaspoons Italian Spice Mix (page 155), or store-bought equivalent
2 cups water

TO SERVE
Grated Parmesan

Select the SAUTÉ setting and heat the olive oil in the pressure cooker. Add the onion and cook for 4 minutes, adding the garlic, salt, pepper, and Italian spice mix during the last minute of cooking. Add 2 cups water, pasta, and tomato sauce (in that order, do not stir!). Secure the lid and place on MANUAL with high pressure for 5 minutes. Quick release and remove the lid. Return the pot to SAUTÉ and add the beans to heat through, about 4 minutes. Serve with Parmesan.

ASPARAGUS AND PARMESAN RISOTTO

I always get so excited to see fresh asparagus in the grocery store in the springtime—it means summer is on the way. To keep that same spring feeling all year, use frozen asparagus in this dish for fresh flavor.

Prep time: 5 minutes | Cook time: 6 minutes (SAUTÉ) + 4 minutes (MANUAL) | Serves 4

PRIMARY INGREDIENTS

One 10-ounce package frozen asparagus, or 2 cups fresh, cut into ½-inch pieces, ends trimmed and discarded
2 garlic cloves, minced, or 1 teaspoon jarred minced garlic
1 teaspoon fresh thyme leaves, or 2 teaspoons dried
1½ cups Arborio rice
3¼ cups vegetable stock

ON-HAND INGREDIENTS

2 tablespoons olive oil
2 teaspoons kosher salt
½ teaspoon freshly ground black pepper

TO SERVE

¾ cup grated Parmesan, for garnish

Select the SAUTÉ setting and heat the olive oil in the pressure cooker. Add the asparagus and cook until slightly soft, about 4 minutes. Add the garlic and thyme and cook for an additional minute. Season with the salt and pepper. Add the rice and stir to coat in the oil, about 1 minute. Add the stock, secure the lid, and place on MANUAL with high pressure for 4 minutes. Quick release and remove the lid. Stir the risotto to combine and garnish with Parmesan.

CHICKPEA CURRY

When I am in the mood for something healthy and clean but full of flavor, this is my dinner of choice. The curry gives the chickpeas a powerful and hearty flavor that makes this a great vegetarian meal.

Prep time: 5 minutes | Cook time: 4 minutes (SAUTÉ) + 4 minutes (MANUAL) | Serves 4

PRIMARY INGREDIENTS
1 cup frozen chopped onion, or fresh chopped onion
2 garlic cloves, minced, or 1 teaspoon jarred minced garlic
3 teaspoons curry powder
½ teaspoon ground ginger
Two 15-ounce cans chickpeas, drained and rinsed
1 cup long-grain white rice, rinsed

ON-HAND INGREDIENTS
2 tablespoons olive oil
2 teaspoons kosher salt
½ teaspoon freshly ground black pepper
1¼ cups water

Select the SAUTÉ setting and heat the olive oil in the pressure cooker. Add the onion and cook until translucent, about 4 minutes, adding the garlic, curry powder, and ginger during the last minute of cooking. Season with the salt and pepper. Add the chickpeas, rice, and 1¼ cups water. Secure the lid and cook on MANUAL with high pressure for 4 minutes. Quick release and remove the lid. Stir to combine and serve.

BLACK BEANS AND RICE BOWL

Beans and rice are the perfect versatile dish for any group of people. Try using different spices, beans, and whole grains to make different flavor combinations for an easy lunch or dinner. I've even used the leftovers as a taco filling the next day.

Prep time: 5 minutes | Cook time: 4 minutes (SAUTÉ) + 3 minutes (MANUAL) | Serves 4

PRIMARY INGREDIENTS

1 onion, chopped, or 1 cup frozen
   chopped onion
2 garlic cloves, minced, or 1 teaspoon
   jarred minced garlic
One 15-ounce can black beans, drained
   and rinsed
1 cup long-grain white rice, rinsed
1½ cups vegetable stock
1 cup jarred salsa

ON-HAND INGREDIENTS

2 tablespoons olive oil
2 teaspoons kosher salt
½ teaspoon freshly ground black pepper
1 tablespoon Mexican Spice Mix
   (page 152), or store-bought equivalent

Select the SAUTÉ setting and heat the olive oil in the pressure cooker. Add the onion and cook until translucent, about 4 minutes, adding the garlic, salt, pepper, and Mexican spice mix during the last minute of cooking. Add the black beans, rice, and stock. Secure the lid and cook on MANUAL with high pressure for 3 minutes. Allow to naturally release for 5 minutes, then quick release. Remove the lid, fluff with a fork to combine.

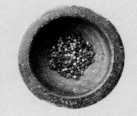

SPICE MIXES & SAUCES

Included in this chapter are recipes for spice mixes, sauces, and condiments that will make your pressure cooking life easier during the week. Make these in advance, keep stored in an airtight container, and you are good to go! Spice mixes will last for up to one year in an airtight container, and sauces for one week in the refrigerator. Making spice mixes and sauces from scratch gives that "homemade" feel, but also keeps the recipe quick and simple to get dinner on the table in no time!

MEXICAN SPICE MIX

I am a huge fan of Mexican food; the flavor is robust and the spiciness adds a kick to any flavor profile that is perfect. Use this spice mix to take your tacos, enchiladas, or chili up a notch!

Prep time: 2 minutes | Yields ¾ cup

PRIMARY INGREDIENTS

¼ cup chili powder

2 tablespoons paprika

1 tablespoon plus 2 teaspoons ground cumin

1 tablespoon garlic powder

1 teaspoon dried oregano

1 teaspoon cayenne pepper

Mix together all the ingredients in a small bowl. Transfer to an airtight container to store for up to 1 year.

GREEK SPICE MIX

Greek dishes are one of my favorite flavor profiles in the summertime. Whether grilled or baked, the lemon and herb flavors bring a freshness that is delicious.

Prep time: 2 minutes | Yields ¾ cup

PRIMARY INGREDIENTS
¼ cup dried oregano
3 tablespoons dried thyme
2 teaspoons dried basil
1 tablespoon garlic flakes
2 teaspoons dried marjoram
2 tablespoons flaky sea salt

Mix together all the ingredients in a small bowl. Transfer to an airtight container to store for up to 1 year.

CAJUN SPICE MIX

Give any dish that spicy, peppery but herby New Orleans flair
with this Cajun spice mix.

Prep time: 2 minutes | Yields ¾ cup

PRIMARY INGREDIENTS
2 tablespoons dried oregano
2 tablespoons garlic powder
¼ cup paprika
1 tablespoon dried thyme
3 teaspoons freshly ground black pepper
1 teaspoon cayenne pepper

Mix together all the ingredients in a small bowl. Transfer to an airtight container to store for up to 1 year.

ITALIAN SPICE MIX

Why buy Italian seasoning when you can make it yourself? Use this seasoning in classic Italian pasta dishes, to sprinkle on pizza crust before layering with sauce and cheese, or in a homemade Italian salad dressing.

Prep time: 2 minutes | Yields ¾ cup

PRIMARY INGREDIENTS

¼ **cup dried oregano**
2 **tablespoons dried basil**
2 **tablespoons dried thyme**
1 **tablespoon dried rosemary**
1 **tablespoon dried marjoram**

Mix together all the ingredients in a small bowl. Transfer to an airtight container to store for up to 1 year.

LEMON HERB SPICE MIX

Entertaining can seem daunting—with this spice mix, everything is changed. Try using this Lemon Herb Spice Mix when roasting chicken (see page 33)—my dinner guests always leave asking for the recipe.

Prep time: 2 minutes | Yields ¾ cup

PRIMARY INGREDIENTS

3 tablespoons dried parsley

1 tablespoon dried lemon zest

2 tablespoons dried thyme

1 tablespoon dried rosemary

2 tablespoons flaky sea salt

1 tablespoon crushed red pepper flakes
   (optional for spice)

Mix together all the ingredients in a small bowl. Transfer to an airtight container to store for up to 1 year.

HERBED BREAD CRUMBS

What I love about this bread crumbs recipe is that it gives an extra buttery, herby crunch to any pressure cooker dish. Definitely keep these on hand in an airtight container to add that oven-baked texture to any pressure cooker recipe.

Prep time: 5 minutes | Cook time: 6 minutes (SAUTÉ) | Yields 2 cups

---

PRIMARY INGREDIENTS
2 tablespoons unsalted butter or olive oil
2 cups panko bread crumbs
2 tablespoons dried parsley, thyme,
   or tarragon

ON-HAND INGREDIENTS
2 teaspoons kosher salt

Select the SAUTÉ setting and heat the butter in the pressure cooker. Add the bread crumbs and salt and cook until golden brown, about 6 minutes. Transfer from the pressure cooker to an airtight container. Stir in the herbs to combine just before serving. Store the bread crumbs for up to 2 weeks in an airtight container.

BBQ SAUCE

BBQ sauce is a staple in my fridge, whether it is used as a condiment or for pulled pork (page 69). This recipe makes it easy to make a homemade BBQ sauce from scratch in minutes.

Prep time: 2 minutes | Cook time: 6 minutes (MANUAL) | Yields 3¾ cups

PRIMARY INGREDIENTS

2 cups ketchup

1⅓ cups cider vinegar

¾ cup dark brown sugar

2 tablespoons Worcestershire sauce

1 tablespoon smoked paprika

ON-HAND INGREDIENTS

⅔ cup water

2 teaspoons freshly ground black pepper

Place all the ingredients in the pressure cooker. Secure the lid and set on MANUAL with high pressure for 6 minutes. Use quick release and remove the lid. Transfer to an airtight container to store for up to 1 week in the refrigerator.

TOMATO SAUCE

I love making a homemade red sauce from scratch, but sometimes that can take several hours! When I'm in a pinch, I make this quick red sauce recipe to have an easy weeknight pasta meal.

Prep time: 5 minutes | Cook time: 2 minutes (SAUTÉ) + 20 minutes (MANUAL)
Yields 7 cups

PRIMARY INGREDIENTS
5 garlic cloves, minced, or 3 teaspoons
   jarred minced garlic
2 teaspoons dried thyme
1 teaspoon dried oregano
Two 28-ounce cans crushed tomatoes
1 tablespoon granulated sugar
1 tablespoon crushed red pepper flakes
   (optional)

ON-HAND INGREDIENTS
2 tablespoons olive oil
2 teaspoons kosher salt
1 teaspoon freshly ground black pepper

Select the SAUTÉ setting and heat the olive oil in the pressure cooker. Add the garlic, thyme, and oregano and cook until fragrant, 2 to 3 minutes. Season with the salt and black pepper. Add the tomatoes, sugar, and optional red pepper flakes and bring to a simmer. Secure the lid and set on MANUAL with high pressure for 20 minutes. Allow to naturally release for 5 minutes, then quick release and remove the lid. Store in clean airtight containers in the refrigerator for up to 1 week or in the freezer for up to 3 months.

CREAM SAUCE

Let's be real: What can go wrong with any homemade cream sauce? This recipe adds the perfect creaminess to the casseroles, pasta dishes, and bakes that are throughout this book.

Prep time: 2 minutes | Cook time: 10 minutes (SAUTÉ) | Yields 3½ cups

PRIMARY INGREDIENTS

4 tablespoons unsalted butter
¼ cup all-purpose flour
3½ cups whole milk

ON-HAND INGREDIENTS

2 teaspoons kosher salt
½ teaspoon freshly ground black pepper

Select the SAUTÉ setting and place the butter in the pressure cooker. Allow the butter to melt and then add the flour. Whisk to form a paste. Slowly stream in the milk and allow to simmer. Add the salt and pepper. Simmer until thickened, 8 to 10 minutes. Transfer to an airtight container to store for up to 1 week.

CREDITS

Pages 4–5, 9, 12, 64–65, 104, 120–21, 150: © Milkos/iStockPhoto.com; pages 10, 151: © Magone/iStockPhoto.com; page 15: © Lilechka75/iStockPhoto.com; page 16: © Elena_Danileiko/iStockPhoto.com; page 19: © rez-art/iStockPhoto.com; pages 20, 28, 72, 76, 105, 113: © bhofack2/iStockPhoto.com; pages 23, 59, 96, 109, 118: © LauriPatterson/ iStockPhoto.com; page 24: © Juanmonino/iStockPhoto.com; page 27: © istetiana/ iStockPhoto.com; pages 31, 47, 129: © AlexPro9500/iStockPhoto.com; page 32: © bekchonock/iStockPhoto.com; pages 35, 142, 164: © ALLEKO/iStockPhoto.com; pages 36, 149: © nata_vkusidey/iStockPhoto.com; page 39: © IslandLeigh/iStockPhoto .com; page 40: © DebbiSmirnoff/iStockPhoto.com; page 43: © ginauf/iStockPhoto.com; page 44: © plyato/iStockPhoto.com; page 48: © manyakotic/iStockPhoto.com; page 51: © AlexeiLogvinovich/Shutterstock.com; page 52: © Barbara Didzińska/iStockPhoto. com; page 55: © bgwalker/iStockPhoto.com; page 56: © PeteerS/iStockPhoto.com; page 60: © -lvinst- /iStockPhoto.com; page 63: © msheldrake/iStockPhoto.com; pages 67, 133: © Plateresca/iStockPhoto.com; pages 68, 99: © VeselovaElena/iStockPhoto.com; page 71: © gwenael le vot/iStockPhoto.com; page 75: © topotishka/iStockPhoto.com; page 79: © SarapulSar38/iStockPhoto.com; page 80: © zeleno/iStockPhoto.com; page 83: © wsmahar/iStockPhoto.com; page 84: © Olha_Afanasleva/iStockPhoto.com; page 87: © vm2002/Shutterstock.com; page 88: © Helmut Selsenberger/iStockPhoto.com; page 91: © ruvanboshoff/iStockPhoto.com; page 92: © juefraphoto/iStockPhoto.com; page 95: © Rimma_Bondarenko/iStockPhoto.com; page 100: © rudisill/iStockPhoto.com; page 103: © rjgrant/iStockPhoto.com; pages 106, 159: © AS Food studio/Shutterstock.com; page 110: © Mizina/iStockPhoto.com; page 114: © OksanaKilan/iStockPhoto.com; page 117: © Lucky_ elephant/Shutterstock.com; page 122: © Bartosz Luczak/iStockPhoto.com; page 125: © nicolesy/iStockPhoto.com; page 126: © Bessapics/Shutterstock.com; page 130: © leyaelena/ iStockPhoto.com; page 134: © iko636/iStockPhoto.com; page 137: © AD077/iStockPhoto .com; page 138: © QuietJosephine/iStockPhoto.com; page 141: © Roxiller/iStockPhoto.com; page 145: © IriGri8/iStockPhoto.com; page 146: © Sohadiszno/iStockPhoto.com; page 156: © Fascinadora/iStockPhoto.com; page 160: © PingPongCat/iStockPhoto.com; page 163: © HandmadePictures/iStockPhoto.com

INDEX

Note: Page references in *italics* indicate photographs.

For information about permission to reproduce selections from this book, write to Permissions,
The Countryman Press, 500 Fifth Avenue, New York, NY 10110

For information about special discounts for bulk purchases, please contact
W. W. Norton Special Sales at specialsales@wwnorton.com or 800-233-4830

Manufacturing by Versa Press
Production manager: Devon Zahn

Library of Congress Cataloging-in-Publication Data

Names: Arnold, Laura, author.
Title: Dinner under pressure : 6-ingredient instant one-pot meals / Laura Arnold.
Description: New York, NY : Countryman Press, a division of
W. W. Norton & Company Independent Publishers Since 1923, [2018] | Includes index.
Identifiers: LCCN 2018028375 | ISBN 9781682683446 (pbk.)
Subjects: LCSH: Pressure cooking. | One-dish meals. | LCGFT: Cookbooks.
Classification: LCC TX840.P7 A75 2018 | DDC 641.5/87—dc23
LC record available at https://lccn.loc.gov/2018028375

The Countryman Press
www.countrymanpress.com

A division of W. W. Norton & Company, Inc.
500 Fifth Avenue, New York, NY 10110
www.wwnorton.com

10 9 8 7 6 5 4 3 2 1